International Cooperation in Research and Development

An Inventory of U.S. Government Spending and a Framework for Measuring Benefits

Caroline S. Wagner

Prepared for the
Office of Science and Technology Policy

Critical Technologies Institute

RAND

PREFACE

This report presents findings from research conducted by the Critical Technologies Institute at RAND as part of the project "Assessing the Costs and Benefits of International Cooperation in Science and Technology." This report

- describes the results of a RAND inventory of U.S. government spending on international cooperation in research and development (ICRD) in fiscal year 1995
- characterizes the nature of ICRD activities
- reports and critiques methods available for measuring the benefits of this activity
- presents a framework of measures that can be used to monitor the benefits of international cooperation in research and development.

The findings herein should be of interest to government policymakers concerned about international relations in science and technology, to government program managers interested in examining the benefits of ICRD, and to those in the science and technology community interested in tracking research and development spending. This project's Web homepage is www.rand.org/centers/cti/stp. For access to the RaDiUS Web page, go to https://radius.rand.org/.

Research and data analysis for this report was conducted by the author, aided by Jennifer Kawata, Kirstin Fisk, and Peter Cannon of the RAND staff. The project was requested by and conducted under the guidance of Deanna Behring, National Security and International Affairs Division, Office of Science and Technology Policy (OSTP), Executive Office of the President. This report has been peer reviewed, and it has been reviewed by the OSTP staff. Conclusions in this report are RAND's alone and should not be ascribed to the Office of Science and Technology Policy.

Created in 1991 by an act of Congress, the Critical Technologies Institute (CTI) is a federally funded research and development center within RAND and was contracted through the National Science Foundation. CTI's mission is to

- provide analytic support to the Executive Office of the President of the United States
- help decisionmakers understand the likely consequences of their decisions and choose among alternative policies

- improve understanding in both the public and private sectors of the ways in which science and technology can better serve national objectives.

Inquiries regarding CTI or this document may be directed to:

Bruce W. Don
Director, Critical Technologies Institute at RAND
1333 H Street, N.W., Suite 800
Washington, D.C. 20005
(202) 296-5000
www.rand.org/centers/cti
cti@rand.org

CONTENTS

FIGURES

TABLES

SUMMARY

The United States spends considerable sums on international cooperation in research and development (ICRD). In fiscal year 1995, for example, the U.S. government spent more than $3.3 billion, which is more than 4 percent of the annual federal research and development budget. The U.S. government maintains 26 bilateral "umbrella" agreements and hundreds of agency-to-agency agreements to support and encourage international cooperation in science and technology. Policymakers have expressed concerns about this cooperative research. Some fear that the United States is paying more than its fair share of the work's cost. Others worry that the country is giving away critical know-how to potential foreign competitors. Additional concerns have been voiced that cooperative programs subordinate the interests of true science to strategic or political ends. These claims are difficult to test for a number of reasons: the large number, varying goals, and long timelines of projects; the underdeveloped nature of tools for measurement; and the lack of a system for linking international science and technology agreements with actual spending on cooperative R&D.

CTI set out to determine if the benefits of ICRD could be measured in real-time in a way that does not require explicit reporting by individual projects. After an extensive database search complemented by agency interviews, we identified some 3,000 projects to use as a basis for an approach to quantifying benefits. Our analysis led us to conclude that the key to identifying benefits lay in understanding the relationship between the purpose of the project and the type of project undertaken. Knowing the rationale behind each type project enables us to predict what kinds of benefits are likely to accrue, which in turn enables us to identify applicable metrics. After constructing an assessment framework and identifying metrics, we applied the framework to a case study—earthquake sciences and seismology—to test its applicability.

PURPOSES OF ICRD

We identified four broad reasons for government to fund an ICRD project:

- If the scale of the equipment or investment required to conduct the project is large.
- If the nature of the subject is global.
- If unique expertise or natural resources involved have a remote location.

- If the mission of the agency involved is to support international cooperation.

We found that the majority of ICRD projects are conducted for the first two reasons: because large-scale investments are required, thus making cost-sharing arrangements with other countries desirable, and because the global nature of the subject lends itself to international cooperation. We identified eight specific activities involved in these types of projects: collaborative research, conferences, contracts (if not classified), database development, operational support, standards development, technology transfer, and technical support. The overwhelming majority of U.S. spending supports the first of these activities, collaborative research (see Figure S.1).

IDENTIFYING ICRD SPENDING

The U.S. government committed at least $3.3 billion in federal R&D spending to projects involving some form of international cooperation in fiscal year 1995. In addition, federal governments agencies spent as much as $1.5 billion in other activities that were not tagged as R&D funds but that constitute scientific or technical activities involving significant international cooperation. NASA leads U.S. agencies in committing funds to ICRD, followed by the Department of Defense, the Agency for International Development, and the Department of Health and Human Services. Multinational activities accounted for more than half of all the spending identified. For

RANDMR900-S.1

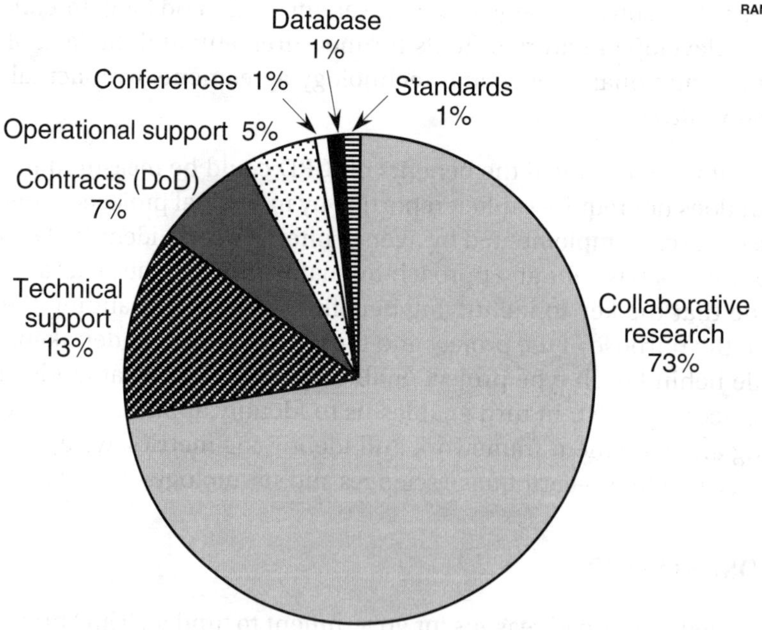

NOTE: Percentages do not add to 100 because of rounding.

Figure S.1—U.S. International Cooperative Research and Development Spending by Nature of Activity

projects in which the United States works with just one other nation, the largest share of the dollars were claimed by projects with Russia. When parsed by field of science, aerospace and avionics was by far the largest area of dollar concentration in a field of science, followed by earth sciences and environment, physics, and health.

Measuring Benefits

Measuring the benefits of these activities requires making the expected benefits explicit and then crafting measures to help enumerate these benefits. At the intersection of the reasons for conducting cooperative research (e.g., the global nature of the research) and the type of research activity chosen (e.g., collaborative activities), expected benefits can be identified. Measures of the results and outcomes of research can provide insight into how well a program is meeting its goals and thereby producing a benefit to the United States. Using available tools to measure outputs and outcomes—bibliometric measures, milestones, surveys, and expert judgment—can provide usable information to help policymakers track the benefits the United States is receiving from ICRD. We describe a framework for applying these measures to different types of ICRD activities.

Seismic Research: A Case Study

In a case study examining cooperation in earthquake sciences and seismology, we tested the ability of the above measures to provide feedback on benefits. Based on the framework of measures developed for this project, we identified three applicable measures: bibliometrics, a survey of research participants seeking information on leveraging foreign research dollars, and expert judgment on standards development. Using these measures, we found that papers co-authored jointly by at least one U.S. national and one foreign researcher had nearly doubled over a 10-year period, with the largest growth being in multinational authorship. The survey found that, on average, the foreign financial contribution equaled the U.S. contribution. The expert judgment standards survey found that the U.S. companies were setting the standard for 80 percent of the essential research equipment used in this field. The measures indicated that the United States is receiving benefits from these activities.

The results of the case study show that the framework can point to possible useful measures. However, improved data on both ICRD spending and outcomes would greatly enhance the ability of decisionmakers to monitor these activities in real time. Government agencies may wish to take advantage of new electronic networking technologies to flag and share data on ICRD activities. In addition, agencies may wish to map ICRD activities against the existing international science and technology agreements to gain a clearer picture of where and why the United States cooperates with other countries on these projects.

Chapter One

INTRODUCTION: RESEARCH, SCIENCE, AND ACCOUNTABILITY

The U.S. federal budget for research and development (R&D) appears likely to decline over the next six years. The American Association for the Advancement of Science (AAAS) projects that federal R&D will decline from $73.7 billion in fiscal year (FY) 1997 to $72.1 billion in FY 2002.[1] This represents a cut of 2.2 percent, or 14 percent after adjusting for expected inflation. This is the largest single decline in the federal R&D budget since the early 1970s. Except for Japan, where plans are in place to significantly expand the public R&D budget,[2] other industrialized nations face similar declining prospects for their national R&D budgets.

As budget deficits and public debt continue to constrain national spending in industrialized nations, policymakers are seeking ways to increase the productivity of the public research dollar. Cooperation among researchers from different countries may provide a way to leverage dollars and increase the productivity of research. The European Union, for example, sponsors the S&T (Science and Technology) Framework Programme to provide opportunities for trans-European cooperation in research that requires investments of a large scale or broad scope. Asian nations also place a priority on international cooperation in science and technology, particularly in areas that support industrial research.

U.S. government policymakers have expressed an interest in increasing international R&D cooperation. In a December 1996 press conference, John Gibbons, Science Advisor to President Clinton, said that as federal R&D budgets shrink, U.S. scientists and program officers should consider expanding international science cooperation as a way to share the cost of developing knowledge, leverage dollars, and increase R&D productivity.[3] While these benefits may accrue to the United States in some cases, they will surely not in every case of international cooperation.

Thus, policymakers need to be able to evaluate when international cooperation is an efficient and effective use of federal dollars. To understand this, policymakers and scientists need to know under what conditions cooperation makes sense, what benefits may accrue to the nation as a result of this activity, and how to monitor benefits

---

[1]AAAS Report XXII: *Research and Development FY 1998,* AAAS and the Intersociety Working Group, Washington, D.C., 1997.

[2]*Science Magazine,* Vol. 275, February 7, 1997, p. 743.

[3]*New Technology Week,* December 9, 1996, p. 1.

over time. Unfortunately, little research exists on ways to track the returns to the nation of investing in R&D, and even fewer studies describe ways to assess the benefits of international cooperation.[4]

PROS AND CONS OF COOPERATING

Science is by nature an international activity, but this doesn't mean that all science benefits from cooperation. In a 1995 report, the congressional Office of Technology Assessment (OTA) stated that "the expanding range of scientific and technological undertakings, and the development of new tools to expedite the exchange of information, have reinforced and augmented the international dimension of scientific inquiry."[5] The OTA study identifies four key reasons why international cooperation in science (at least for factors leading to an increase in "big science," the subject of the OTA study), makes sense:

- The pooling of intellectual and technical resources from throughout the world has led to important breakthroughs in a variety of fields.
- Cooperation enhances the ability to draw on competencies of other nations and gain access to foreign facilities.
- Large-scale projects may be too big for a single nation to undertake.
- Domestic and international political considerations often serve as important reasons to cooperate on specific projects.[6]

However, the logistics of cooperating with colleagues from around the world is almost always more difficult and more expensive than participating in domestically-based research. Time differences and language barriers complicate communications, physical distance makes travel expensive, and different levels of national commitments to project funding may reduce the efficiency or increase the risk of joint projects. International projects may sometimes require significant and possibly duplicative equipment purchases in the United States and abroad. Moreover, if the United States is leading in an area of science, there may be less incentive for the United States to share knowledge and resources with other countries, at least in some fields.

The OTA study also identified a number of limitations to participating in international collaborative projects, including the following:

- There is difficulty in guaranteeing the long-term financial commitment by all project partners.

---

[4]One relevant study is *Techniques and Methods for Assessing the International Standing of U.S. Science*, Caroline Wagner, Santa Monica, Calif.: RAND, MR-706.0-OSTP, 1995.

[5]U.S. Congress, Office of Technology Assessment, *International Partnerships in Large Science Projects*, OTA-BP-ETI-150, Washington, D.C.: U.S. Government Printing Office, July 1995, pp. 11–12.

[6]Ibid.

- The collaborative process may inhibit innovation by limiting competition among researchers.
- Large international projects require elaborate management and decisionmaking mechanisms.
- Cooperation may lead to the loss of commercial advantage through the transfer of leading-edge national technologies.[7]

THE LARGER TREND TOWARD ACCOUNTABILITY

The financial and scientific motives for increasing international cooperation are colliding with the national debate surrounding the issue of quantitative assessment of government research and development programs. The debate about measuring research and development arises in the context of a government-wide trend toward public accountability for the benefits received for dollars spent. Several recent events have shifted the attention of government program managers from focusing *ex ante* at justifying budgets and *ex post* at evaluating programs, toward continuous tracking and monitoring of activities using performance measures. This trend is motivated in part by a similar change in industrial management practices. Continuous tracking and monitoring received its largest boost in the summer of 1993, when the U.S. Congress passed the Government Performance and Results Act (GPRA) "to improve the efficiency and effectiveness of Federal programs by setting goals for program performance and measuring results."[8] The Act urges federal agencies to shift from an input focus to "an emphasis on performance and results."[9] These requirements are also contained in the Clinton Administration's National Performance Review.[10] Federal government agencies are testing new management practices and preparing to report program-based strategic plans, milestones, and outcome measures as part of the FY99 budget cycle.

The task of continuous tracking and monitoring of R&D outputs and outcomes is particularly arduous because these programs' progress is hard to anticipate and their results are difficult to predict and measure. Moreover, the results of scientific research are often an intermediate product—new knowledge—which is then applied to reach other goals. As the National Science and Technology Council (NSTC) has noted in its report on assessing fundamental science: "Science proceeds through a slow process of accretion of results. Major breakthroughs do not necessarily occur on a regular basis, and an essential element of scientific research is the replication of

---

[7]Ibid. p. 13.

[8]Report of the Committee on Governmental Affairs, United States Senate, to accompany S. 20, *Government Performance and Results Act of 1993,* U.S. Government Printing Office, June 16, 1993, 103rd Congress, 1st Session, Report 103-58, p. 2.

[9]Leon E. Panetta, *Memorandum for the Heads of Executive Departments and Agencies,* M-94-2, Executive Office of the President, Office of Management and Budget, October 8, 1993.

[10]Vice President Al Gore, *From Red Tape to Results: Creating a Government that Works Better and Costs Less,* report of the National Performance Review, Washington, D.C., September 7, 1993.

earlier findings in order to confirm or generalize them."[11] Existing measures described briefly in this report, and more fully in other RAND publications cited later, can capture important elements of research output, but, as the NSTC has noted, significant aspects of research cannot be quantified using straightforward measurement techniques.[12]

Although scientific research is hard to quantify, measures do have a place in understanding the benefits of international cooperation, particularly those related to new knowledge creation. Moreover, international cooperation has a number of goals beyond the creation of new scientific knowledge that provide possibilities for measurement. In addition to the creation of new scientific knowledge, goals for scientific activity, such as access to data and equipment, improved world health, enhanced political relations, and national defense and security, provide fields for measurement. However, ICRD activities are not easily identifiable in traditional budget reporting; activities are decentralized and dispersed throughout the government. Collecting these activities together for the purpose of measuring benefits requires crafting a methodology and criteria for identification.

BOUNDARIES, SCOPE, AND METHODOLOGY OF THIS STUDY

This study examines government spending on international cooperation in research and development (ICRD) and attempts to draw from, regroup, and augment existing assessment methods to create a framework for measuring the benefits of ICRD on a real-time, continuous basis.[13] Because of the diversity and range of the ICRD activities being studied, analytic boundaries have been drawn for the purpose of conducting this study, focusing on

- actual cooperative activities rather than international agreements to cooperate
- research and development budget obligations rather than on the less clearly defined category of "science and technology"
- award and project activities counted from the "bottom-up," rather than relying on one-time reports from various agencies
- the creation of a transparent and reproducible approach to assessment, rather than relying on anecdotes of success.

---

[11]National Science and Technology Council, *Assessing Fundamental Science,* Committee on Fundamental Science, July 1996, p. 4.

[12]Ibid., p. 7.

[13]Research and development is a budget term used by the Office of Management and Budget and applied within government agencies to define a specific form of federal investment activity. In fiscal year 1995 this activity amounted to approximately $70 billion. Only those activities classified by federal agencies as "R&D" are included in this inventory. We recognize that projects and activities outside of the defined set of "R&D" projects might be considered to be scientific or technical in nature, but to ensure consistency, we do not include these activities in this inventory.

Actual Activities Versus International Science and Technology Agreements

International science and technology agreements (ISTAs) can be an important indicator of national interest to cooperate in R&D. In fiscal year 1995, the United States government had 26 active "umbrella" or "framework" ISTAs signed at the White House level. These agreements provide the protocol for sharing scientific data and equipment, exchanging researchers, and conducting collaborative projects. In addition to the framework agreements, the Department of State's Title V Report cites over 850 agency-to-agency bilateral and multilateral agreements to conduct international cooperative research, provide technical support, or share data and/or equipment. Fourteen agencies have signed international science and technology agreements with 71 countries and 2 regions (the European Union and a consortium of African countries) in 22 fields of science and technology. Most agreements are bilateral: In the 1995 Title V report, 651 of the agreements reported were signed by the United States and one other nation. Multilateral ISTAs accounted for 116 of the signed agreements.

It has been widely assumed that ISTAs constitute the scope of U.S. ICRD activities. In fact, ISTAs are non-funded, diplomatic-level agreements that have no associated budget authority. Many ISTAs are never fully implemented because of lack of funds from one or more parties. On the other end of the spectrum, individual investigators often collaborate with their international peers without reference to the existence of an ISTA. Relying on the list of ISTAs can actually be misleading when the goal is identifying the range and character of ICRD actually being funded by the U.S. government. Accordingly, this study identifies federally funded ICRD projects regardless of whether they were sponsored by or were otherwise a part of a government-to-government ISTA. While we were aware of the many ISTAs in place to encourage international cooperation, we did not use these as a guide to find ICRD activities. Rather, we sought to identify actual, on-going, federally funded international cooperative activities.

Research and Development Versus Science and Technology

In popular literature, the terms "science and technology" and "research and development" are sometimes used interchangeably, but, within the U.S. federal government, they have very different meanings. R&D is a specifically defined budget category, constituting the $70+ billion often referred to in government and policy publications when discussing the government's investment in science and technology.[14] The federal government's $70+ billion R&D investment is split between defense research, which claims half or more of the total R&D budget, and discretionary funding at more than a dozen research and mission-oriented agencies.

---

[14]For example, the 1995 National Academy of Sciences report (*Allocating Federal Funds for Science and Technology,* issued by the Committee on Criteria for Federal Support of Research and Development, National Academy of Sciences, National Academy of Engineering, Institute of Medicine, and the National Research Council) uses "R&D" and "S&T" almost interchangeably throughout the report.

The Office of Management and Budget (OMB) defines R&D activities within the federal budget in Circular A-11 as activities falling within these general guidelines:

- Basic research—systematic study to gain knowledge or understanding of the fundamental aspects of phenomena and of observable facts without specific applications toward processes or products in mind.
- Applied research—systematic study directed toward greater knowledge or understanding necessary to determine the means by which a recognized and specific need may be met.
- Development—application of knowledge toward the production of useful materials, devices, and systems, or methods, including design, development, and improvement of prototypes and new processes to meet specific requirements.

OMB allows individual agencies some latitude in determining which activities constitute the conduct of R&D. Each agency may use its traditional, historic definitions of R&D when reporting R&D activities to OMB. As a result, each federal agency defines the "stages" (basic, applied, and development) of R&D in the context of its particular mission. This results in variations among the agencies as to what constitutes basic and applied research and development.

Agency variations in accounting for R&D result in data that are often difficult to compare. The OMB definitions of R&D specifically exclude the training of scientific and technical personnel. However, the support of research assistantships for Ph.D. research is sometimes included in the "conduct of R&D" as a grant provided by an agency to a scientific researcher. Moreover, R&D data may differ across agencies in the accounting for salaries and indirect costs: These may be included or excluded from the total R&D budget, depending upon the nature of the research or the vehicle for its funding.

Among the agencies, the Department of Defense (DoD) has the most unique approach to accounting for R&D. The DoD reports seven stages of R&D to OMB: DoD budget categories 6.1–6.3 correlate with the OMB definitions for basic, applied, and development R&D—DoD refers to all three categories as "S&T." The DoD delineates budget categories 6.4–6.7 as testing, evaluation, and design activities—DoD refers to these four categories as "R&D." The federal government's $70+ billion R&D budget comprises all seven DoD 6.1–6.7 activities' budgets.

Specifically not counted as R&D within the U.S. government budget are endowments, such as the U.S.–Israel Science and Technology Commission; capital investment, such as the Global Seismographic Network; routine product testing; quality control; mapping; collection of general-purpose statistics; experimental production; routine monitoring and evaluation of an operational program; and the training of scientific and technical personnel. Some of these activities might be considered S&T by a reasonable observer and may involve some international cooperative activities, such as collecting, tracking, and reporting weather data. Nevertheless, these activities are not budgeted as R&D so that they cannot be compared across agencies or tracked from year to year.

The particularities of federal budgeting terms and practices have important implications for this study. To create an inventory of international R&D spending that is comparable across agencies and over time, this project used government R&D budget dollars because these are identifiable, comparable, and traceable data.[15] Figure 1.1 illustrates how the terms are used and where this study has focused its efforts. Figure 1.1 also shows how, in an effort to make the data comparable across agencies, we eliminated the DoD 6.4–6.7 data from this inventory, since these activities generally involve testing and evaluation activities not conducted under R&D budgets in other agencies.

The collection and assessment methods used in this study are designed to allow reproducible and comparable results across a number of cases. The study included four phases: First, we conducted an inventory of government spending on international cooperation in R&D in FY95.[16] Second, we developed a notional list of benefits that might be expected to accrue to the United States in the process of conducting the types of international cooperation in R&D identified in phase one. Third, we examined possible measures for assessing the benefits of these activities, and, with this list, we constructed a framework that matches benefits to measures in a way that would elicit real-time quantitative and qualitative information on ICRD activities. Finally, we conducted a case study to test whether the framework and the suggested measures provided practical, policy-relevant information. This report presents the findings from and analysis of these four phases of the project.

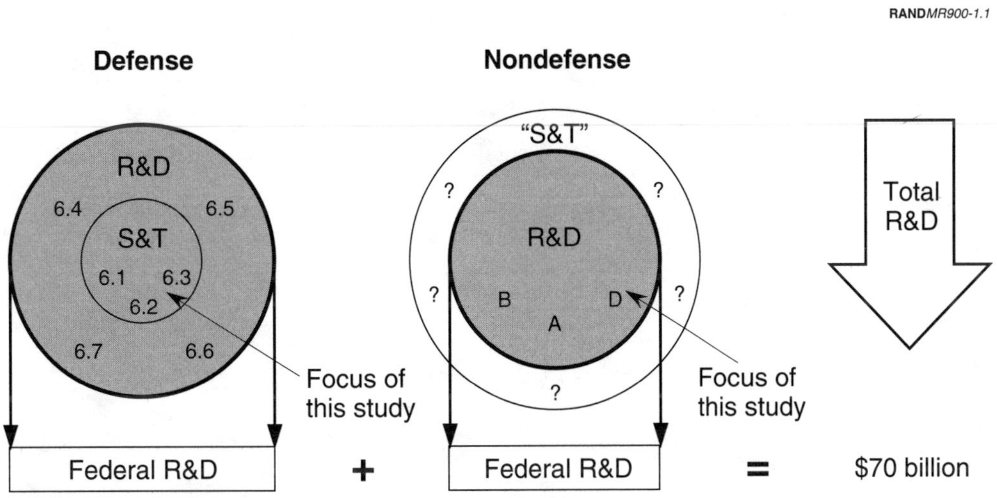

Figure 1.1—"Research and Development" Versus "Science and Technology"

[15]The case study described in the appendix sought to include all S&T activities without regard to R&D budgetary classification.

[16]The U.S. federal government's fiscal year begins on October 1 and ends on September 30.

ORGANIZATION OF THIS REPORT

Following this introduction, Chapter Two describes the data collection process: The methodology used for this study is unique, and understanding it is central to interpreting the results of the study. Chapter Three contains the quantitative results of the inventory of FY95 government spending on international cooperation in R&D as well analysis of the data. Chapter Four presents a framework for assessing the benefits of ICRD and describes a case study that used the assessment framework as a guide. Chapter Five concludes with remarks on the need for and ways to improve data collection on international cooperation. Appendix A contains summary tables of the data we collected. Appendix B is output from RAND's Web page of RaDiUS, outlining U.S. government programs that report ICRD.

Chapter Two

INVENTORY METHODOLOGY

No one set of government activities easily comprises the category "international R&D cooperation." Activities vary by agency mission, by country, by topic, and by many other variables. Conducting an inventory of ICRD requires significant detective work that includes reading thousands of individual program, project, and award data contained within RaDiUS or obtained from agency sources. The process for collecting data and the criteria for inclusion are presented here. Our findings are presented in Chapter Three.

SOURCE OF THE DATA

The vast majority of data on government R&D spending is electronically available and fully searchable through RAND's RaDiUS database, the first comprehensive, fully searchable data system that contains information on the approximately $70 billion of annual spending classified by the federal government as "research and development," as defined by OMB Circular A-11.

Identifying the Data Set

Figure 2.1 shows the five steps taken to create this inventory. Part one involved collecting data from official and primary data sources. The RaDiUS database and supporting data tables were searched using an iterative search strategy. Searches were conducted on words (such as "international" in conjunction with "collaboration"), on units of government (such as NASA), and on countries and continents (such as "Japan" or "Asia"). Hundreds of searches were run to capture all relevant programs, projects, and awards. Part two of the process generated abstracts of candidate programs, projects, and awards.

Part three involved examining and sorting the data and running additional searches where needed. Once the full set of relevant activities was identified, we read the project descriptions and award abstracts, and, with reference to the criteria established for this study, rejected or counted the project in the inventory and classified the activity according to a range of characteristics. Over 9,000 program and project descriptions and award abstracts were read. Many of the 9,000 were not relevant to the study but were captured in the searches because they had terms such as

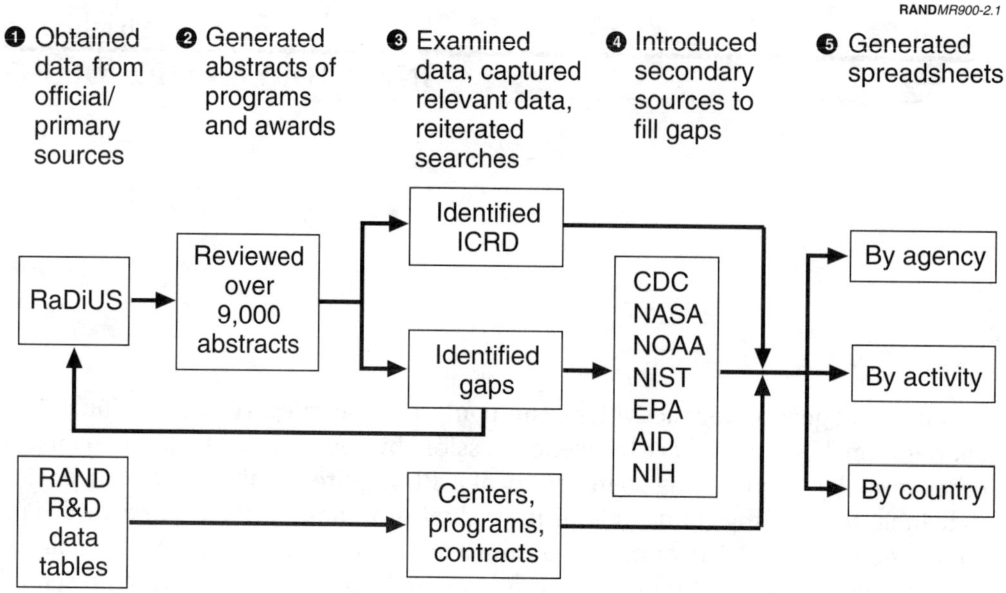

NOTES: CDC is Center for Disease Control; NASA is National Aeronautics and Space Administration; NOAA is National Oceanic and Atmospheric Administration; NIST is National Institute of Standards and Technology; EPA is Environmental Protection Agency; AID is Agency for International Development; and NIH is National Institutes of Health.

Figure 2.1—Method Used to Compile Data

"international implications" or "international reputation." In addition, many terms, such as "Japanese maple," Chinese hamster," and "New Zealand rabbit," were inadvertently captured. Once these awards and projects were eliminated from the data set, the inventory data set numbered approximately 3,000 projects and awards.

Part four of the process involved consultations with federal funding experts and with staff at the Office of Science and Technology Policy to identify where additional data were needed. We then contacted government officials to ask for assistance in validating data obtained from RaDiUS, and if necessary, in identifying additional budget data. In some cases, supplementary data were not available from the agency. (These cases are noted in the agency descriptions in Chapter Three.) Part five of the process involved compiling all the data collected from all sources, placing the data in spreadsheets and examining the data for duplications and obvious errors, then coding and analyzing the data set.

Refining the Data Set

Included in this inventory are any type of program-based activity—projects or awards (contract, grant, or cooperative agreement)—that have, as *one of the principal purposes,* the sponsorship of international cooperation. Clearly, there is much international activity, coordination, and sharing that is not captured by this inventory since we limited the study to activities where cooperation is a specific project

goal. If a project or award description reported cooperation as a principal purpose, the *full average annual* FY95 budget authority[1] for that activity was included in the inventory. While this method may have led to overcounting in a limited number of cases, the alternatives were unworkable. Alternatives could have included (1) asking agency officials to report on the share of a project dedicated to R&D—a datapoint they usually do not have available, (2) contacting principal investigators directly and asking them to report on the extent of funding dedicated to ICRD—a Herculean task given the final data set of nearly 3,000 projects, or (3) having RAND staff make a judgment—an impossible task without additional information.

Cooperation is defined for the purposes of this study as federally supported activities where a U.S. government-funded researcher is involved in a project with a foreign researcher, a foreign research institution, a multinational institution, or a multinational research project. Projects and awards that fell within this definition encompassed scientist-to-scientist collaboration as well as cases of field research where a scientist worked with a collaborator to gain access to a natural resource, research for a Ph.D. dissertation when that activity was classified by the agency as "R&D," and cases where government agencies support the conduct of research through operational and technical support, again, where that activity is counted as R&D. The definition did not include activities for which a U.S. government official met for a brief time or intermittently shared data with counterparts from other countries.

Agencies that use contracts, grants, and cooperative agreements to conduct most or all of their research and development are the most fully represented in the RaDiUS database and therefore are the most fully represented in this inventory. When government money changes hands, records are made of those transactions, and the grant or contract recipient often provides a full description of the activities. This is often referred to as extramural research. Agencies that primarily sponsor extramural research include the National Science Foundation (NSF),[2] Health and Human Services (HHS),[3] the U.S. Department of Agriculture, and the non–lab-based activities of the Departments of Defense and Energy (DoD and DoE). If international cooperation was established after the grant or contract was awarded, the activity will not be captured by this search methodology.

When the R&D is conducted within government laboratories—intramural research—spending is more difficult to track. While we made an effort to identify and characterize these activities, ICRD activities in these parts of the government may not be fully represented in this study. Identifying and collecting information on intramural research involved first using RaDiUS to locate the likely federal agencies that contain these activities, and second contacting the agencies to seek the information directly. Even though we made extensive efforts to contact agencies with program or lab-based activities, at times it was difficult to decouple the international activities from other activities going on in these agencies or laboratories. (In two cases—NASA and

---

[1]In many cases, the activities identified in this inventory were funded on a multi-year basis. In these cases, RaDiUS reports, and the project team counted, the average annual funding figure.

[2]Close to 95 percent of NSF R&D funds leave the agency in the form of grants or contracts.

[3]Close to 80 percent of HHS RD funds leave the agency in the form of grants or contracts.

the Smithsonian—we worked with the agencies to identify the international components of programs.) Agencies sponsoring this intramural activity include parts of NASA, the EPA, the Agency for International Development (AID), the DoD, the DoE, and the Smithsonian Institution.

Coding the Data Set

As the full data set was being compiled, the data were coded four ways:

- By country, or, in cases where researchers from more than two nations are involved or where a U.S.-funded researcher reported working with a multinational research organization, as a "multinational" activity.
- By type of cooperation, in categories developed by RAND, for identifying the character of the ICRD projects or programs funded by the U.S. federal government, as shown in Table 2.1.
- By fields of science or technology, using a list, shown in Table 2.2, adapted by RAND from the National Science Board list of areas of science and technology.
- By sponsoring agency.

STRENGTHS AND LIMITATIONS OF THIS APPROACH

The data collection technique used in this study has significant strengths. First, the data have been gathered from the "bottom up" by identifying activities at the lowest level and aggregating up into programs, bureaus, and agencies. Second, this approach enabled consistent screening of the data using a single filter. This helped us ensure the comparability of data across agencies. Third, this approach has the advantage of identifying ICRD activities in actual operation as opposed to cooperation merely proposed in international bilateral and multilateral cooperative agreements. Fourth, the method we used is transparent and reproducible. This allows trend analysis over time and across agencies.

The approach used to conduct this inventory also has limitations. Some agencies do not compile or report data on activities at the project or award level. In these cases, the inventory includes only program-based activities at highly aggregated budget line items. AID, for example, reports data only at the budget line item, so no additional analysis or comparison of AID activities is possible. The AID budget line item data are delineated by region, but that is the most detailed data we could find for AID activities. When this inventory was performed, AID could not provide additional information on the types of R&D activities sponsored in these regions. The EPA also does not report detailed project-level activities. A small amount of DoE and DoD lab-based activities may also be unreported.

Table 2.1

Types of Cooperative Activity Identified in the Course of the Study

Collaboration	Research activities where a principal purpose of the activity is to sponsor international collaboration of the following types: between a researcher funded by the U.S. government in a joint project with a collaborator from another country, where a researcher funded by the U.S. government is conducting a research program that involves actively sharing information with another researcher conducting the experimental or observational research, or where a researcher is contributing to an international cooperative project. (Not where a U.S. researcher is using international data or data from another country, not where a U.S. researcher is training foreign students in the United States or another country, and not where U.S. graduate students are studying in another country.)
Conference	Either foreign or domestic—and including symposia, workshops, or other official meetings where scientists from around the world participate in a scientific or technical meeting to describe and share ongoing research.
Contracts	Where the U.S. government contracted with a foreign source for the purpose of conducting research and development.
Database development	Where the U.S. government is sponsoring the creation of an international database of information being collected from sources worldwide, and which will be available to researchers from around the world.
Operational support	Where the U.S. government is funding the building, maintenance and/or operation of an international research center, designed specifically for the purposes of international collaboration, in the United States or in a foreign country.
Standards development	Where the U.S. government is sponsoring the development of a technical or scientific standard that will serve as the basis for future research, development, or production for practitioners around the world.
Technology transfer	Where the U.S. government is actively seeking to transfer technology from a foreign country to the United States.
Technical support	Where a U.S. government laboratory or a U.S. government-sponsored researcher is providing research and development results or other support to a foreign researcher or laboratory.

Table 2.2

Fields of Science Used to Identify the Nature of ICRD

Physical Sciences	Engineering Sciences	Life Sciences	Social Sciences
Mathematics	Chemical Engineering	Plant Biology	Economics
Physics	Computer Engineering	Agricultural Sciences	Anthropology
Chemistry	Communications Engineering	Biotechnology	Demographics
Earth Sciences	Materials Technology	Biomedical Technology	Other Social Sciences
Geology	Aerospace and Aeronautics	Environmental Sciences	
Other Physical Sciences	Other Engineering Sciences	Other Life Sciences	

Chapter Three

RESULTS OF DATA COLLECTION: FEDERAL GOVERNMENT SPENDING ON INTERNATIONAL COOPERATION IN RESEARCH AND DEVELOPMENT

The U.S. federal government spent approximately $3.3 billion on projects involving international cooperation in research and development in fiscal year 1995.[1] This amount constitutes 4.5 percent of the $70+ billion of government R&D spending in FY95. Ten agencies of government actively supported more than $1 million of ICRD. Over 100 countries are listed as a partner, or as the location, for cooperative research activity. Cooperation spans most areas of science and technology but is heavily concentrated in aerospace research and the earth sciences.

This chapter presents the results of our data collection and analysis. The analysis focuses on

- the character of the ICRD
- the share of ICRD going to multinational and binational activities
- international partners in binational R&D
- fields of science represented in ICRD
- agency by agency support for ICRD
- mechanisms for conducting ICRD.

THE CHARACTER OF INTERNATIONAL COOPERATION IN RESEARCH AND DEVELOPMENT

Collaborative research is by far the largest single ICRD category being funded by U.S. government agencies. Figure 3.1 shows the breakdown by the character of the activity classified for the purposes of this analysis.

[1]This includes only one-fourth of the funding appropriated for the International Space Station, even though, in its essential mission, the space station is an international project. However, much of the R&D for the International Space Station is done by U.S. researchers, and including the total $1.9 billion of Station funding skews the final number and misrepresents the extent of international research activities.

RANDMR900-3.1

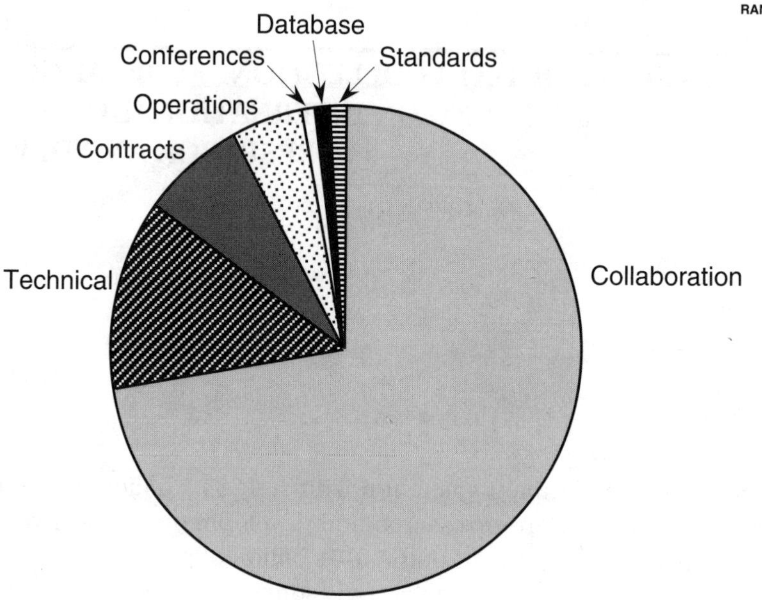

Figure 3.1—Spending by Nature of Activity

- The overwhelming majority of activities: 73 percent, were judged to be *collaborative* in nature, where U.S. scientists and foreign scientists work together on a common research program, project or research problem. Funds are spent in the United States, in foreign countries, or in both places.
- *Technical* support, where the U.S. government funds the application of our own scientific or technical know-how to aid a foreign country with domestic problems, was 13 percent of activities. Much of this funding is spent outside of the United States.
- DoD *contracts,* set aside as a separate category because of their unique nature, accounted for 7 percent of the spending.
- *Operational* support, where U.S. funds support centers of international research, accounted for 5 percent of funds.
- *Database development, standards development,* and *conferences* together accounted together for less than 3 percent of funded activities.

Multinational and Binational ICRD Activities

Multinational cooperation claims $2 billion of the $3.3 billion we identified as ICRD activities. Multinational spending dominates ICRD because of the huge financial investments required by "big science" projects such as a space station, global climate research, fusion research and other high-energy physics activities, polar research and ocean drilling, and health-related research in such areas as human genome and infectious disease control.

Binational projects account for about $1.3 billion of FY95 ICRD spending. Figure 3.2 illustrates the share of binational cooperation by country. Funding for binational cooperation was approximately $8 million or less with each of the following countries: Russia, Australia, Japan, Canada, the United Kingdom, Israel, China, and Mexico. All parts of the world are represented in binational research, as illustrated in Figure 3.3: Countries in Eastern Europe account for the largest regional share (39 percent), because of spending on research with Russia; Asia accounts for 18 percent of binational cooperation; Western Europe accounts for 15 percent, and all other regions account for 10 percent or less of U.S. government funding on binational cooperation. Table 3.1 shows regional spending by agency.

Binational Research

ICRD with Russian scientists and Russian research institutes accounted for the largest share of ICRD binational spending: Over $100 million was spent on binational cooperative research with Russia alone. NASA accounted for the largest amount of cooperative spending on projects with Russia, followed by ICRD projects funded by the Department of Defense and the Department of Energy. These projects focused heavily on space-based life support, nuclear waste containment, energy storage, and environmental pollutants. U.S.-funded cooperative research with Russia led to the filing of at least 16 inventions with the U.S. Patent and Trademark Office between 1991 and 1996.

RANDMR900-3.2

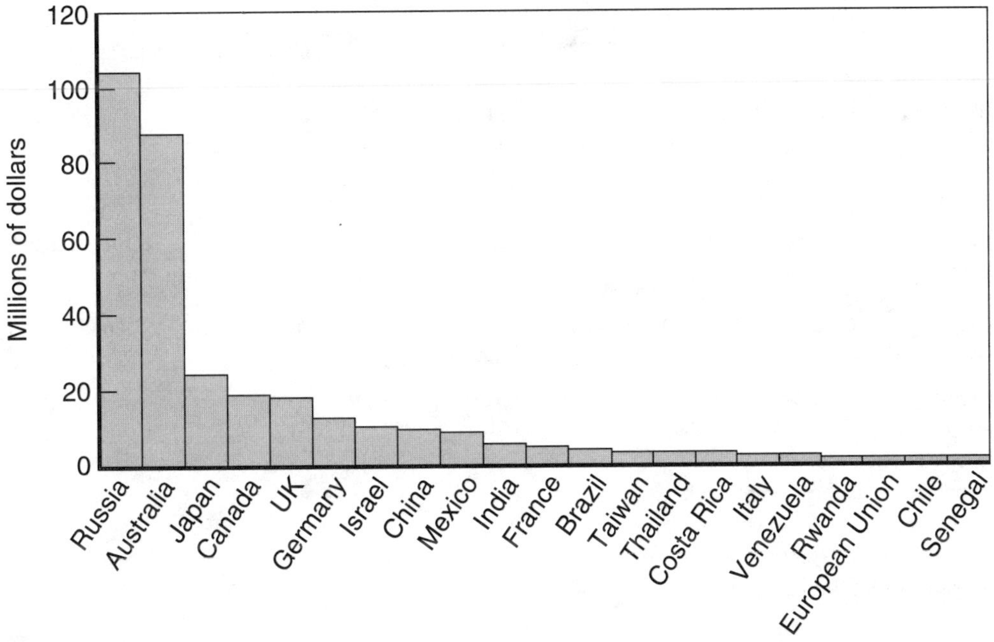

Figure 3.2—Binational Cooperation by Country

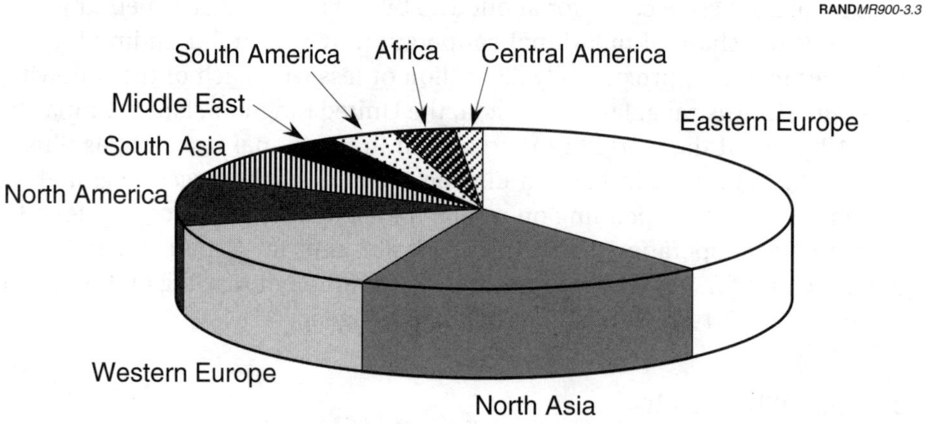

Figure 3.3—All Parts of the World Are Involved in ICRD

Table 3.1

Agency Spending, by Region (in dollars)

Agency	Africa	Asia	Eastern Europe	Middle East	North America	Oceania	Russia & FSU[e]	South/ Central America	Western Europe	Other
AID	73,343	17,019	11,250	8,509	0	0	11,250	20,758	0	0
DoC[a]	50	189	0	0	46	0	145	152	0	2,241
DoD	0	667	0	6,372	115	83,342	9,703	341	14,372	349,681
DoE	0	17,174	0	0	1,070	177	7,330	0	8,062	87,201
EPA	0	174	0	0	344	0	429	160	0	3,500
HHS	7,531	28,253	680	3,342	15,449	1,571	754	6,203	4,102	4,070
NASA	0	183	0	63	1,063	83	80,875	60	831	190
NRC[b]	0	0	0	0	0	0	0	0	0	0
NSF	1,693	16,678	938	528	4,253	3,373	4,269	5,765	8,101	129,066
Smith-sonian	0	0	0	0	0	0	0	0	0	27,750
USDA[c]	0	157	0	409	3,871	444	578	138	200	1,006
DVA[d]	0	539	0	0	406	0	47	446	411	0
Grand Total	82,617	81,031	12,869	19,224	26,618	88,989	115,381	34,025	36,079	604,705

[a]Department of Commerce.
[b]Nuclear Regulatory Commission.
[c]U.S. Department of Agriculture.
[d]Department of Veterans' Affairs.
[e]Former Soviet Union.

Australia's presence in the top eight cooperating countries, with $88 million of ICRD spending, is the result of several large DoD contracts to conduct R&D with Australia on a shared control and ground station satellite system that will be located in Australia. Without the DoD contracts, Australia would not be on the top-10 list of primary ICRD binational partners. Aside from the DoD contracts, NSF funds about $2.8

million in cooperative research with Australia, and HHS cooperates in about $1.6 million of research with Australian scientists.

Binational ICRD with Japan, totaling $24 million, focused on energy research and earth sciences. The Department of Energy and the National Science Foundation accounted for the largest shares of funding for cooperative projects when Japan was our sole partner. Joint U.S. government-funded research with Japan led to at least 11 patents being filed by U.S. government agencies over the six year period of 1991–1996.

Other nations represented included the following:

- Cooperation with Canada totaled $18 million in FY95, dominated heavily by Canadian researchers working with NIH researchers.
- Cooperation with the United Kingdom ($17 million), Germany ($11 million), and Israel ($9.6 million) is led by the Department of Defense; beyond this binational cooperation with DoD, cooperative activity between these three countries and the United States ranges across a number of different agencies.
- Cooperative research with Mexico, totaling $9.6 million, is heavily focused on agricultural research funded by the USDA, followed by cooperation with NIH and NSF, focusing on agriculture and health research.
- China's FY95 $9 million binational ICRD is focused on research with NIH and NSF.

Fields of Science Represented in ICRD

Aerospace, avionics, and aeronautics accounts for more than half of the bulk of research dollars committed to a single field of science, as shown in Figure 3.4. A distant second to aerospace are the combined fields of the earth sciences (including geosciences, natural resource research, and environmental research), which, when added together, make up 15 percent of all ICRD activities—the second largest category behind aerospace.

The next largest category—physics—is 5 percent of ICRD activity spending. Less than 5 percent each are biomedical and biology, followed by engineering and materials, and other social sciences. Figure 3.5 shows how spending on sciences is distributed when aerospace is removed.

AGENCY SUPPORT FOR ICRD

Ten agencies dedicate significant portions (more than $1 million each) of their federal R&D budgets to international cooperative activity. These are, in descending order of total ICRD spending: NASA, the Department of Defense, the Agency for International Development, the National Science Foundation, the Department of Energy, Health and Human Services, the Smithsonian, the Environmental Protection Agency, the U.S. Department of Agriculture, and the Department of Commerce. A break-

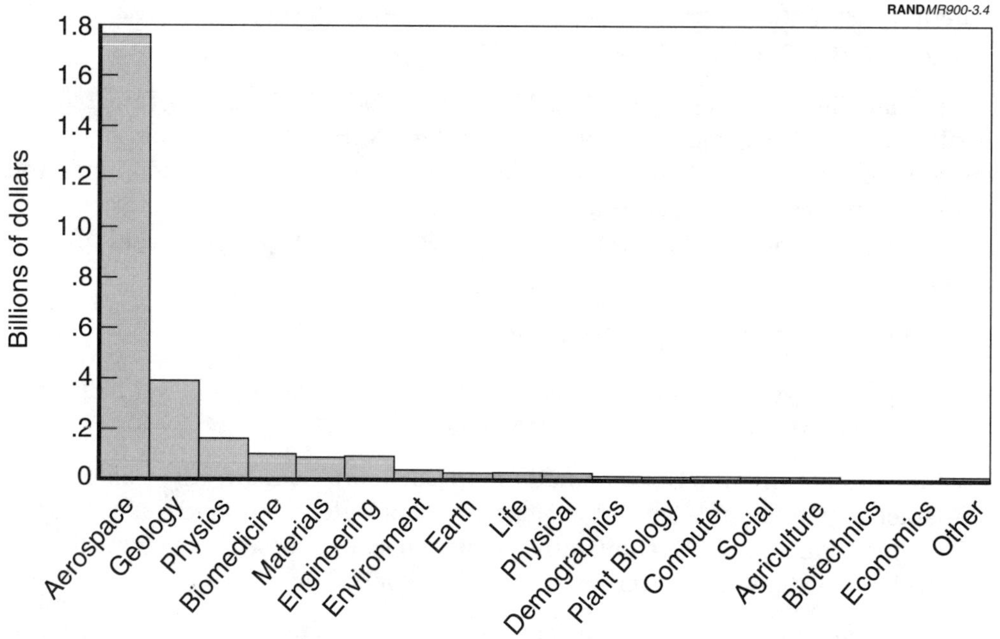

Figure 3.4—Cooperation in Areas of Science, Including the Area of Aerospace

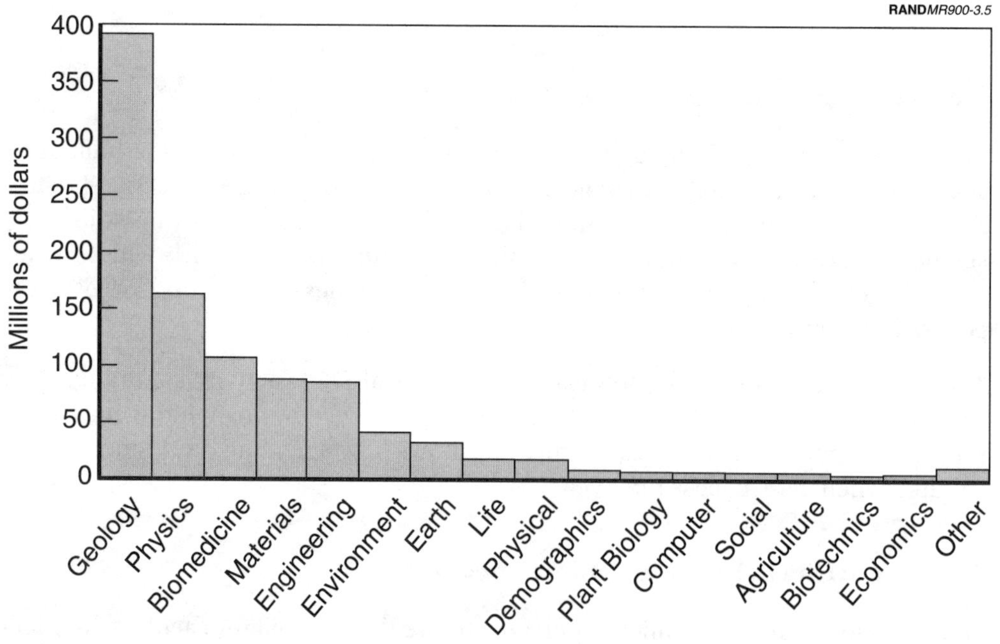

Figure 3.5—Cooperation in Areas of Science, Excluding the Area of Aerospace

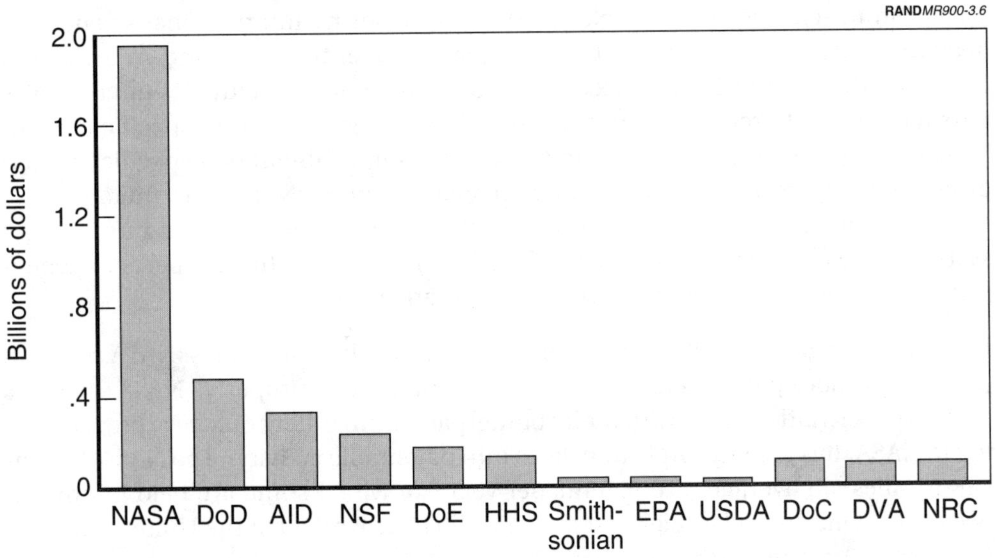

Figure 3.6—Agency ICRD Funding, Including NASA Funding

down of agency-by-agency funding is shown in Figures 3.6 and 3.7. Appendix A contains a summary table showing the breakdown by agency and by program.

National Aeronautics and Space Administration (NASA)

NASA leads government agencies in total ICRD dollars spent: approximately $1.9 billion, or 20 percent of its total R&D spending, is devoted to ICRD activities. International cooperation is a charter mission of this agency.[2] Activities such as the International Space Station, the Cassini Satellite Program, Mars '94, Earth Observing Satellite System, and the advanced space transportation program are funded by Congress with the understanding that these activities will be conducted in cooperation with foreign space agencies and international entities.

The programs within NASA that have the greatest commitment to ICRD are Mission to Planet Earth, Space Science, the International Space Station, the Space Shuttle, and Life and Microgravity Science. The International Space Station represents a very large portion of NASA's R&D budget. In our consultations with NASA, it was decided that this inventory should count only one-fourth of the Station's total program budget toward the total. NASA's main international partners include countries with advanced space programs: Russia, Japan, France, the United Kingdom, Germany, Canada, Brazil, and also the European Space Agency.

In FY95, NASA reported 60 international agreements to the Department of State (Title V Report). The agreements were signed by NASA to encourage and support co-

---

[2]The summary table in Appendix A lists the legislative authority for NASA's international science and technology cooperation.

operation in science and technology. When sponsoring international science endeavors, NASA's work involves the exchange of scientific data and information. When building systems and spacecraft, NASA's collaborative activities often involve parsing out to different partners the research and development of specific components of large systems or cooperating on the accomplishment of a specific mission originating either at NASA or in a foreign space agency. NASA's partners provide specific components to NASA, and the final product is incorporated into a larger system, spacecraft, or mission. Each of the international partners expects to benefit from the scientific data generated by the cooperative efforts.

Because of the nature of its international cooperative R&D activities, NASA research does not produce jointly held invention-based intellectual property. NASA scientists co-author scientific papers with their counterparts from other countries, but, according to NASA, this activity rarely translates into patentable activity. The NASA Administrator files, on average, 110 patents per year,[3] of which some are held jointly between U.S. citizens and foreign researchers who have worked in the United States on NASA-sponsored research.

Department of Defense (DoD)

The Department of Defense devotes a significant amount of funding to ICRD, $450 million in FY95, but the intensity of ICRD activities is low compared with its FY95 R&D budget of $36 billion. The ICRD counted in this inventory was limited to those

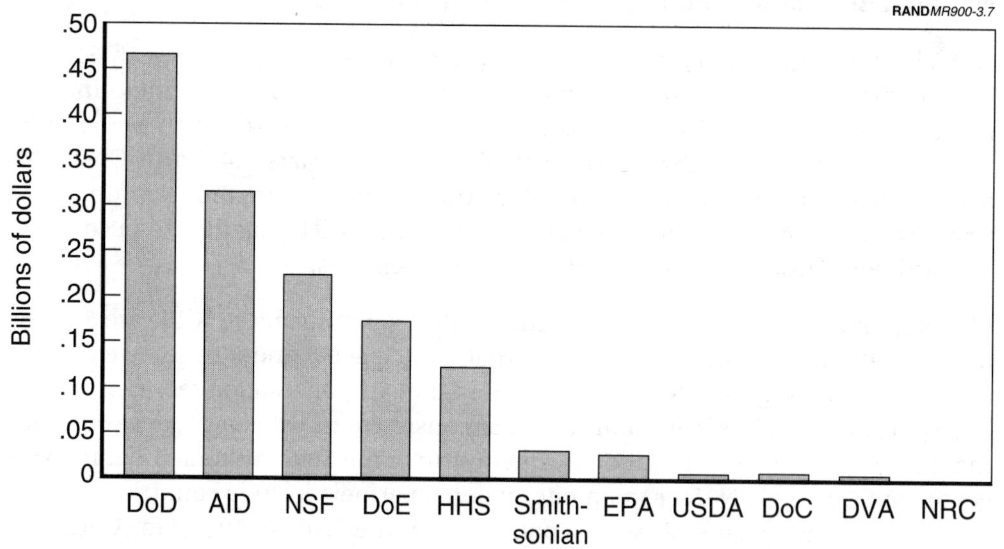

Figure 3.7—Agency ICRD Funding, Excluding NASA Funding

[3]This number is some fraction of the patents that result from NASA-sponsored work. Under U.S. law, contractors who invent a new product or process may retain rights to an invention for the purpose of commercializing this invention, even if it is developed with government money.

activities classified by DoD as 6.1–6.3, which are roughly equivalent to the OMB's basic and applied research and development categories.[4] The low level of DoD's ICRD intensity may be due largely to the absence of a mandate for DoD to conduct R&D jointly with other countries, in contrast to that of NASA or the National Science Foundation. The Department of the Army leads other DoD units in its commitment to international cooperation, with over $240 million in ICRD spending, followed by the Air Force, the Navy, and the Advanced Research Projects Agency. The Ballistic Missile Defense Organization, the Defense Nuclear Agency, and the Department of the Navy also commit approximately $1 million each to international cooperation.

DoD's international cooperative activities are dominated by a number of large contracts (more than $10 million) granted to foreign companies or research institutes to conduct R&D on large systems, such as missiles and space systems. In addition to its contracting activity, DoD laboratory-based researchers undertake joint scientific research with foreign counterparts for scores of small projects. DoD ICRD joint efforts were conducted primarily with researchers from the United Kingdom, Australia (satellite system development), Russia, Israel, and various European countries.

DoD has entered into hundreds of bilateral agreements to conduct joint research. The Department of the Army alone has over 300 letters of intent and memoranda of understanding about international scientific cooperation or agreements to share equipment with other nations.[5] Between 1991–1996 DoD's ICRD resulted in the filing of at least 12 patents with the U.S. Patent and Trademark Office.

Agency for International Development (AID)

The Agency for International Development's mission includes conducting R&D with, and for the benefit of, third country partners.[6] Accordingly, we included all of AID's FY95 R&D funding of $313 million toward the ICRD inventory. AID spends the bulk of its R&D money, $162 million, on global issues such as infectious disease, disaster prevention, and environmental issues. Spending on research with, for, or in Africa represents the bulk of AID's regional spending ($73 million), followed by spending in Asia ($25.5 million), Europe/the Commonwealth of Independent States (CIS) ($22.5 million), and Latin America and the Caribbean ($20.7 million). AID does not break down its budget below these broad categories, nor are project descriptions available, so additional analysis of AID activities was not possible for this study.

National Science Foundation (NSF)

Among the government agencies, NSF has by far the most varied and extensive support for projects with an international component. While the total amount of funds

---

[4]The Department of Defense reports seven stages of R&D to OMB as part of its accounting for the $36 billion: 6.1–6.3 correlates with the OMB definition of basic, applied, and development. 6.4–6.7 accounts for testing, evaluation, and design activities.

[5]The summary table in Appendix A lists the legislative authority for this activity.

[6]The summary table in Appendix A lists the legislative authority for this activity.

being spent on projects featuring scientific cooperation, $220 million, does not approach NASA or DoD levels, NSF's activities represent 10 percent of that agency's FY95 R&D spending of $2.2 billion, making NSF a highly ICRD-intensive agency.[7] Moreover, in terms of total numbers of projects, NSF exceeds most other agencies. NSF funds hundreds of small grants to researchers taking part in collaborative research, technical data exchange, or conferences with foreign researchers. NSF reported 15 bilateral ISTAs with foreign countries to the Department of State in 1995. When scientific projects were conducted on a binational basis, major collaborators on NSF-funded projects were Russia, Japan, Germany, France, Canada, India, and the United Kingdom. Since 1991, NSF's ICRD activities have resulted in the creation of at least 10 reported inventions.

In addition to funding grants that support ICRD, NSF funds the operation of four centers that serve as focal points for international research: the National Astronomy and Ionospheric Center, the National Center for Atmospheric Research, the National Optical Astronomy Observatory, and the National Radio Astronomy Observatory. These centers house researchers from around the world and provide data that support the work of scientists in dozens of countries. NSF's contribution to "big science" projects includes funding ocean drilling and polar research.

Within the NSF directorates, Geosciences leads other directorates in funding projects for international collaborative functions, awarding grants of over $28 million to international activities, an amount representing 7 percent of total R&D funds for this directorate. Geosciences supports large international projects such as ocean drilling, global climate change, and scores of smaller projects on earthquake sciences and seismology.

The Directorate on Social, Behavioral & Economic Sciences follows closely behind Geosciences in total commitments to projects with an international component, in large part because this directorate contains the Division on International Cooperative Scientific Activities, a division of NSF with FY95 R&D spending totaling $15.8 million. Mathematical and Physical Sciences also contributes significantly to ICRD activities, devoting more than $12.5 million to international research in physics alone. The Directorate on Biological Sciences spends nearly $10 million on international environmental and biological studies.

Department of Energy (DoE)

The Department of Energy (DoE) spent $180 million in international cooperation on high-energy physics, nuclear waste containment, and energy storage and generation. DoE's ICRD spending is a small portion of its FY95 R&D budget of $6 billion. DoE's official report to the Department of State on bilateral cooperation cites 54 international science and technology agreements to conduct ICRD in effect in 1995. The agency's international office reported to RAND that DoE has active more than 500 in-

---

[7]This amount also does not include capital investment projects that NSF has funded in other countries, nor does it include education and training moneys spent on international projects, since these expenditures are not accounted for as R&D.

ternational science and technology agreements at the treaty and subtreaty level. Unlike most other agencies, DoE has statutory authority[8] to enter into executive level cooperative agreements, such as those supporting ICRD, without requesting approval from the Department of State. When DoE projects involved just one other nation, Japan, Russia, and Germany were DoE's largest partners. DoE's official ICRD activities since 1991 have resulted in at least 23 patentable inventions.

Within the departmental programs, High Energy and Nuclear and Plasma Physics programs committed the largest amount to projects involving international cooperation, at about $20 million. These programs include commitments to the International Thermonuclear Experimental Reactor, a large international fusion research project.

Among DoE's contract laboratories, 13 list programs or projects that involved cooperating with foreign researchers or research institutes. Due to the nature of DoE's research, there may be additional international cooperative activities not captured in this inventory—for example, foreign scientists often spend months or years at DoE labs, but these activities would not be counted in this inventory. In addition, DoE laboratory scientists may be working with foreign partners on specific unreported projects. Among the projects we identified at the labs, Argonne National Laboratory's research base had the largest number of projects with foreign partners, with cooperative research programs accounting for more than $35 million. Sandia (ICRD—$22 million), Lawrence Livermore (ICRD—$24 million), and Pacific Northwest (ICRD—$15 million) Laboratories also had significant international cooperative research activities.

Department of Health and Human Services (HHS)

Among the agencies of HHS, the National Institutes of Health (NIH) spends the largest amount on projects involving international collaboration and cooperation. Other HHS agencies participating in ICRD are the Centers for Disease Control (CDC) and the Agency for Health Care Policy and Research. In 1995 HHS reported 61 executive-level agreements for conducting bilateral research to the Department of State. In addition, the agency annually signs scores of letter agreements with foreign governments to exchange information and equipment.

NIH's international cooperative programs and projects total more than $110 million in FY95 R&D funds. Included in this total is the FY95 R&D funding of $14.2 million for the Fogarty International Center to support a range of international cooperative research projects, conferences, and educational activities. Among the institutes, the top five ICRD spenders are the National Cancer Institute (ICRD—$22 million), the National Heart, Lung, and Blood Institute (ICRD—$13 million), the National Institute of Allergy and Infectious Diseases (ICRD—$13 million), the National Center for Research Resources, and the National Institute of Child Health and Human Develop-

[8]The summary table in Appendix A lists the legislative authority for this activity.

ment (ICRD—$6 million). These institutes are also among the top eight institutes in NIH's funding in the FY95 budget.

The ICRD spending figures for NIH do not necessarily include the amounts spent on the activities in which foreign scientists take part in NIH laboratory-based research. In 1995, NIH hosted more than 3,000 foreign scientists as visitors or guest researchers to conduct research. Recall that unless the program reported international cooperation as a principal focus of research, it was not counted toward the total inventory. Accordingly, all of NIH's international collaborative activities are not represented in the inventory total.

CDC spent close to $15 million of its $217 million FY95 R&D budget on international cooperative projects. In addition to direct spending on ICRD, CDC provides reimbursable support to other countries on infectious diseases and epidemiology that is only partly reflected in the $15 million total. The Agency for Health Care Policy and Research also spent about $2 million on ICRD activities.

HHS researchers collaborated most often with researchers representing Canada, China, Japan, Israel, and Europe. Since 1991, HHS-sponsored intramural ICRD has resulted in the filing of at least 10 patents.[9] Extramural research, which accounts for about 80 percent of NIH's R&D funds, has resulted in hundreds of patents held by private and university-based researchers, an unknown number of which may be the result of international cooperation.

Smithsonian Institution

Although not a government agency, the Smithsonian Institution received a direct appropriation of $136 million in FY95 federal government R&D funds, of which a significant portion went to support ICRD projects and the operation of laboratories for the conduct of cooperative research. In consultation with Smithsonian staff and on examination of Smithsonian's budget, we estimate that the Smithsonian committed about $30 million to ICRD in FY95. The majority of this funding was spent in the Smithsonian's Science Programs, specifically the Smithsonian Tropical Research Institute, located in Costa Rica, and in the International Environmental Science Program. The Smithsonian also funds an international center for research and development and maintains the Canal Zone Biological Area Fund in Panama—both centers of international scientific research. The Smithsonian has registered with the Department of State two executive-level agreements to conduct joint scientific activities.

---

[9]Patent applications list the *current* address of the inventor. In an uncountable number of cases, foreign researchers residing in the United States listing a U.S. address and participating in NIH research have co-filed patents with U.S. citizens. This makes counting foreign co-inventors very difficult. Thus, the number of patents resulting from ICRD conducted in NIH labs is almost certainly understated.

Environmental Protection Agency (EPA)

The Environmental Protection Agency participates actively in the Global Climate Change project to facilitate international scientific data exchange and cooperative research. In FY95, EPA devoted $26 million to ICRD, of which $25 million was dedicated to some aspect of global climate change research. This activity was managed largely by EPA's Air Quality division. The Toxic Substances and Water Quality divisions also sponsored ICRD activities. In 1995, EPA reported to the Department of State that it had 24 ISTAs in place. Over the past six years, EPA has registered three patents that resulted from international cooperative research.

U.S. Department of Agriculture (USDA)

The USDA has an extensive international program that includes ICRD activities sponsored in or with other countries. In FY95, the USDA sponsored about $7.5 million in international cooperative research activities through five bureaus: the Cooperative State Research, Education and Extension Service; the Forest Service; the Foreign Agricultural Service; the Animal & Plant Health Inspection Service; and the Agricultural Research Service. The majority of USDA support took the form of grants to university-based researchers and technical support funds for international cooperative research. In 1995 the USDA reported 30 ISTAs to the Department of State. When USDA projects were conducted on a binational basis, those countries that accounted for the greatest dollar amount were Mexico, Russia, New Zealand, and Israel.

Department of Commerce (DoC)

The Department of Commerce has a comparatively modest FY95 R&D budget—$1.2 billion—of which $4 million was devoted to some form of international cooperation activities at the National Institute for Standards and Technology (NIST) and the National Oceanic and Atmospheric Administration (NOAA). As for the NIH, this amount understates the total international cooperation and consultation between NIST and NOAA researchers and their foreign counterparts. NOAA's ICRD activities account for the bulk of the Department of Commerce international cooperative activities. NOAA spent close to $2.5 million on ICRD in FY95. This funding contributed to global climate change research, ocean drilling research, and hurricane research.

In contrast to the small amount of funds spent on ICRD, the Department of Commerce reported to the Department of State the largest number of international science and technology agreements—299—of any of the R&D-sponsoring agencies. These ISTAs are memoranda of understanding with other countries to conduct data exchanges. In addition, DoC ICRD spending was the most productive of any R&D agency, accounting for 33 patents from 1991 to 1996—the most of any agency examined in this study. The patents resulting from international cooperation sponsored by DoC were mainly registered by scientists from NIST.

Other Agencies

Smaller federal R&D agencies also conduct ICRD or share scientific data as part of their science and technology program. In FY95 the Department of Veterans' Affairs sponsored about $2 million of ICRD in its Medical and Prosthetic Research division. The Department of the Interior (DoI), which had 102 ISTAs[10] in effect in FY95 with 46 countries and two regions, committed R&D funds of about $380,000 for ICRD in earthquake sciences and hazard prevention. In FY95 the Nuclear Regulatory Commission, which reported 73 agency-level ISTAs with 32 countries and two regions for the 1995 Department of State Title V Report, contributed $12,000 for international nuclear safety research.

MECHANISMS FOR CONDUCTING ICRD

The majority of government-funded R&D—between 50 and 90 percent depending upon the agency—is performed under government contract or grant and takes place in laboratories outside of the government. Contractors and grantees tend to be in the private and academic sectors, thus the majority of federally supported ICRD is conducted by private or academic researchers. Other parties conducting ICRD are government agencies, such as AID, and government employees, such as NIH researchers who have foreign collaborators.

ICRD is funded in five ways: (1) through program based activities, such as research within NASA labs that support an ICRD program; (2) through awards—contracts, grants, and cooperative agreements; (3) by funding and maintaining the operation of centers for international research, such as the Smithsonian tropical research center or NSF's atmospheric lab; (4) through funds provided or reimbursed by foreign countries, such as funds provided to a foreign researcher to participate in a U.S. Geological Survey project or funds paid to the Centers for Disease Control to conduct infectious disease testing side-by-side with African research scientists; and (5) funds paid in remission of debt held by the United States, such as the P.L. 480 funds available for USDA research with India. The way in which the government funds ICRD reflects the nature of the benefit that the government expects to receive from the activity. This is discussed in detail in the next chapter.

---

[10]DoI international agreements largely covered the installation of the global seismographic network (GSN), an FY95 $20 million government investment in a network of seismic monitoring sites being paid for by the National Science Foundation and the Air Force. Capital investments like the GSN are not included in government R&D spending data.

Chapter Four

A FRAMEWORK FOR ASSESSING BENEFITS

An assessment of outcomes that is designed to provide feedback in real time requires that government policymakers and program managers develop and apply meaningful and dependable measures. In the past, R&D has been assessed *ex ante*, using peer review or cost/benefits analysis, or *ex post*, using bibliometric measures or technical review. These measures were valid at the two ends of the spectrum, but tools to assess ongoing activities and performance (as required by GPRA) have not been well developed, in part because there has not been much demand for them and in part because scientific activity is so difficult to measure. Nevertheless, R&D activities by law now must attempt to apply quantitative measures, in part to defend the use of scarce federal funds. Providing a framework within which to apply available measures to real-time assessment is the challenge addressed here.

This study tests two important assumptions: first, that *ex ante* and *ex post* measures of scientific activity can be adapted to ongoing research and, second, that to apply these measures, the character and the goals of the research must first be made explicit. This study further seeks to test whether the character of the research reveals the goals of the activity. Benefits expected from ICRD are often not stated up front but may be implicit in the character of the research and the type of research mechanism (i.e., collaborative technical support and so on) chosen to fund and conduct the research (i.e., contract, grant, U.S. government laboratory). When goals are made explicit, the reasons and types of cooperation can help enumerate the expected benefits. Once it is known what benefits are expected, it may be possible to craft measures to determine whether the nation is reaching its goals and receiving the expected benefits.

Assessing the benefits of ongoing ICRD requires matching the reasons and types of ICRD with appropriate measures. Available measures, generally used to report the *outcomes* of R&D—when placed in the proper context—can provide real-time, usable information about the benefits of ICRD. This chapter describes a framework for identifying specific measures that can assess the benefits of ICRD and describes the results of a case study testing this premise.

DEFINING MEASURABLE BENEFITS

This study has identified a number of characteristics of ICRD that can help shed light on expected, measurable benefits. These include (1) the mission of the funding

agency; (2) the character of the research (collaboration, conferencing, etc.); (3) the reasons for choosing ICRD (large scale, global nature, etc.); and (4) funding. The funding mechanism chosen by an agency—grant, contract, cooperative agreement, or program-based activity—reflects the benefits that government expects to derive from the activity:

- Grants and technical support are intended to benefit the receiving party; no direct product or service is expected by the funding agency. NSF grants to researchers promote the conduct of science, not to meet technical specifications of an NSF mission, but to advance excellence in science. USDA grants or aid to Brazilian soybean farmers directly benefits Brazil, with an indirect benefit (lower cost products, perhaps) accruing to the United States.
- Program-based, contract-supported activities are done for the direct benefit of a government's mission-oriented program. Activities such as the manufacture of satellites is often conducted under contract for DoD or NASA to meet their specific technical needs.
- Under a cooperative agreement, both the government and the cooperating party expect to benefit from the activity. University-based efforts under a cooperative agreement to create an international science database for the government is an example of a case where both sides benefit from government R&D funds dedicated to a specific project.

In general, ICRD is funded, not to promote international cooperation, but to meet direct and indirect and long- or short-term goals of the funding agency. In Figure 4.1, the agencies funding ICRD are notionally arrayed along an axis of benefits and goals on one hand and time on the other. Agencies are placed on a discrete point along the axis based on a subjective judgment of the character of that agency's ICRD. Pointers suggest a trend in either the indirect or the long-term nature of that agency's activities. This illustration suggests ways to think about which agencies have programs that would benefit from enhanced quantitative assessment of ICRD. Clearly, different assumptions of how agencies, or different programs within agencies, conduct ICRD could change that agency's place on the axis.

- In the first third of the benefits/time axis, where ICRD projects have a short-term, direct benefit, government agencies often use contracts or intramural research as the method of funding ICRD. In these cases, ICRD is conducted to meet a direct need of the government, for example, the development of a satellite, a prosthetic device or a component for a flight simulator. Government expectations, and notably, the ways to measure the results of these activities, are usually explicitly stated in the contract and quickly measured and evaluated on the basis of the product received.
- In the distant third of the benefits/time axis are technical support activities or grants that may pay off either far into the future, or may never pay off in the sense of creating a measurable outcome. These activities include AID or USDA grants that support foreign scientific, technological, health, or agricultural research or development, which have little or no direct benefit accruing to U.S.

citizens or a government agency, or in some cases, even to the United States, except perhaps in the form of political good will. Because of the indirect nature of the benefits and the generally long time period it takes to produce results, benefits in this far area are extremely difficult to measure. Governments usually undertake this type of activity for reasons of principle, for strategic political reasons, and to support human rights. Defining measures for these activities may not be possible or realistic.

- In the middle third of the benefits/time axis are activities designed to produce a benefit to the U.S. government or U.S. citizens. This is the field we explore in this chapter of the report—where measures can provide some insight, but where benefits have rarely been measured in the past. It is in this middle third that many of the questions of accountability will be discussed in the public forum, and where agencies will need to present new data under emerging government requirements for outcome-based management. Activities in this tier are dominated by grants but can also include intramural, extramural, and contract-supported research.

MEASURING OUTCOMES

In the process of conducting research and development, researchers create products. The products can be new knowledge published in conference journals, a scientific or technical product such as a new chemical catalyst, or a commercial product such as an electronic sensor. The creation of new knowledge and its use by others create "footprints" that provide a way to track the benefits of research and development to

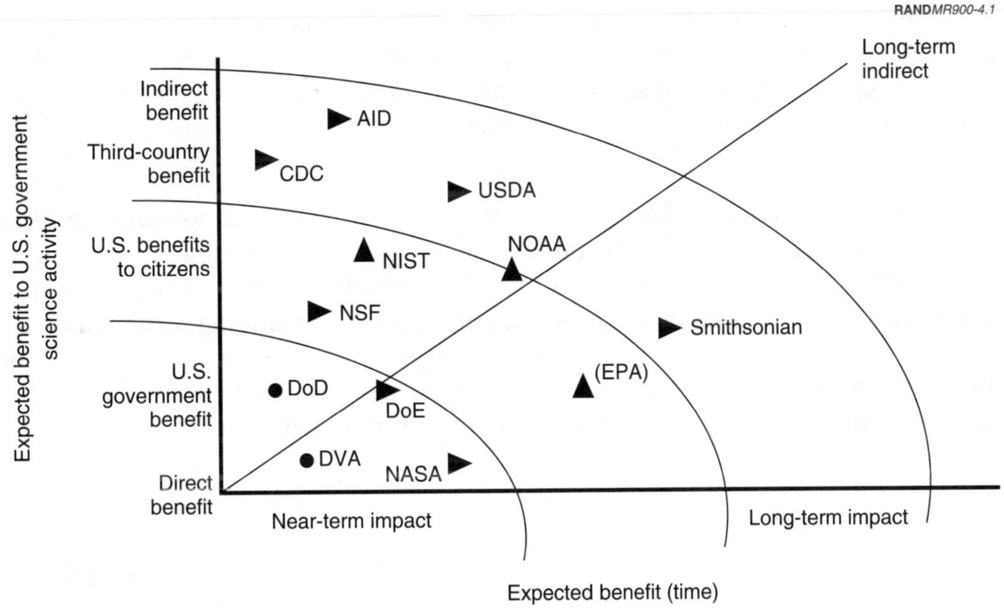

Figure 4.1—Goals/Benefits Arrayed Against Time

science, the economy, the nation, and international relations. The footprints—article citations, patents, product sales, international conferences—can be documented to varying degrees, depending upon the nature of the "product." When compared with expectations or the performance of similar activities in the same or other fields, a measure of the footprints can provide feedback to policymakers and program managers.

Measures of the results and outcomes of research and development can paint a picture of how well a program or project is meeting its goals, and thereby producing benefits for the United States. The "proper context" for using these measures almost always requires a quantitative report of the quality and benefits of research, along with the quantitative measure of footprints. Measures of the output and outcome of research and development are difficult to apply across the board: not all measures will apply in all situations. Measures must be matched to the nature of the activity being assessed.

A FRAMEWORK APPROACH

In an effort to describe measures for ICRD, we have developed a framework to identify first the benefits and then the measures that may shed light on the extent to which the United States is receiving these benefits. The framework developed for measuring the benefits starts with the four broad reasons identified earlier for conducting ICRD: (1) the very large scale of the equipment or investment required to conduct a project; (2) the global nature of the subject; (3) the location of unique expertise or natural resource; and (4) a miscellaneous category, where it is the agency's mission to support international cooperation. For each of these reasons for funding ICRD, projects are crafted to achieve the government's mission. To simplify the list of cooperative projects, we boil these reasons down to four basic types: (1) collaborative research, (2) technical support for a U.S. project or for a foreign S&T project, (3) operational support of a facility to conduct international cooperation, and (4) standards and database development.

At the intersection of the reasons for conducting international cooperation in R&D and the types of cooperation, a list of expected benefits can be enumerated. Arrayed in a matrix, these reasons and types of projects provide the opportunity to identify the nature of the benefit that the government expects from funding ICRD. Once we identify benefits, we can more easily match measures to the nature of the activity being measured. Tables 4.1 and 4.2 present the benefits implied by the government funding at the intersection of the reasons and types of cooperation.

TOOLS FOR MEASUREMENT

Tools available to track and monitor research and development projects, and by extension, ICRD activities, fall into four broad categories: (1) bibliometrics, (2) milestones, (3) surveying, and (4) technical judgment.[1]

- *Bibliometrics* is the technical name for a range of analytical methods using published materials (books, reports, patents, software, designs, prototypes, and blueprints) to develop descriptive statistics, multidimensional analyses, and graphical representations of the output of science. Bibliometrics can take a number of technical data sources for analysis, including the following:
  - Publication counts
  - Citation counts
  - Co-citation analysis
  - Co-word analysis
  - Scientific mapping.
- *Milestones.* Scientific or technical projects often establish "milestones," or achievements, expected over the course of a project. The project team can map these milestones against actual achievements, thereby providing useful information about the outputs of an ICRD project.
- *Technical Review.* Technical or expert review is the most widely used approach in research evaluation, both in the United States and around the world. In the United States, technical review varies among agencies, from very informal assessment processes to highly structured retrospective quality control mechanisms. Within one review, then, the process transforms the descriptive judgments of peers into quantitative ratings, which can be compared across projects to identify those that need improvement.
- *Survey Methods.* Traditional survey methods—either on paper, in person, or by phone, where a group of participants or stakeholders are asked to provide responses to a set of questions—are often used to assess the benefits or outcomes of research.

The differences among the agencies and the range of the nature and character of research and development in the various fields of science and technology make it difficult to craft and recommend measures that will apply equally to all areas of ICRD. A range of measures must be considered. Under NASA programs, for example, programs tend to fall within two broad categories: scientific data exchange and technical cooperation. Neither of these types of activities require a great deal of scientist-

---

[1] We do not include a discussion here of the social returns to research and development because this method is used to assess the benefits of R&D on a broad scale, not at the program or project level. For a full description of social rates of return analysis, see Steven W. Popper, *Economic Approaches to Measuring the Performance and Benefits of Fundamental Science*, Santa Monica, Calif.: RAND, MR-708.0-OSTP, 1995, and Caroline S. Wagner, *Techniques and Methods for Assessing the International Standing of U.S. Science*, Santa Monica, Calif.: RAND, MR-706.0-OSTP, 1995.

Table 4.1

Benefits Expected from and Measures Suggested for Collaborative Research and Technical Support

Reasons for Cooperation	Collaborative Research		Technical Support	
	Expected Benefits	Suggested Measures	Expected Benefits	Suggested Measures
Very large scale equipment	Enable conduct of large-scale project beyond reach of any one country; gain access to foreign equipment; lower cost of research (e.g., space station; ITER; CERN[a])	Agency report on meeting milestones; survey participants for foreign $ and/or in-kind contribution; expert judgment of technical feasibility/excellence; survey records; U.S. percentage of time accessing equipment	Improve opportunities for U.S. scientists, improve efficiency of research equipment, data (e.g., aid in building/maintaining a tropical research lab in Costa Rica)	Extent of usage per sq ft of facility compared with use of a similar domestic facility; extent to which research conducted is published/cited; development of data used in published reports
Global nature of subject	Access to subject of study; leverage scarce funds; improve environment or reduce hazards (e.g., CGC,[b] Ocean drilling, earthquake research)	Survey scientists: gaining access to subject/data. Survey agencies/investigators: leveraging foreign funds. Citation search: no. of co-authored papers increasing. U.S. report: reducing specific hazards in U.S./the rest of the world	Improve capability of U.S. data collection; reduce environmental hazards; improve agricultural efficiency; coordinate data collection (e.g., helping Brazil reduce pollution emissions)	Agency report on usefulness of data; increased crop production; reduced emissions; agency report on coordination of data collection/sharing
Unique foreign expertise	Enable excellent science; share data; improve productivity of research; improve U.S. science base (e.g., French excellence in materials science)	Citation counts of jointly published articles compared with nat'l counts; biblio counts of increased improve productivity of unit of knowledge produced; joint patent counts	Build foreign science capabilities to improve science overall (e.g., working with French scientists in Africa to contain disease)	Agency report on ability of national scientists to manage labs; increased foreign publications/citations; increased joint projects/publications
Government/agency mission	Either meet direct need of agency for new knowledge (e.g., energy) or improve foreign security or living conditions (e.g., DoE's energy security, AID/CDC's aid for infectious disease control)	Use biblio/cite counts to show accessing best knowledge in world; expert judgment or reduced risk; U.S,/other int'l org indicators of improved living conditions	Improve foreign standards of living; reduce infectious disease; improve foreign agriculture (e.g., AID's support for clean water)	U.S./UN data on indicators of standards of living; expert judgment of improved containment of nuclear waste in states of the CIS

[a]Originally, Conseil Européen pour la Recherche Nucleaire. Now known as the European Laboratory for Particle Physics.

[b]Cucurbit Genetics Cooperative.

Table 4.2

Benefits Expected from and Measures Suggested for Operational Support and Standards/Database Development

Reasons for Cooperation	Operational Support		Standards/Database Development	
	Expected Benefits	Suggested Measures	Expected Benefits	Suggested Measures
Very large scale equipment	Provide place for int'l collaboration or cooperation; enable sharing of data (e.g., NSF's astronomical lab)	Extent of usage of facility compared with use of a similar domestic facility; extent to which research conducted is published/cited; development of data used in published reports	Establish global standards that allow cooperative research or commerce; enable access to data to increase research efficiency (e.g., standards for satellite production and signaling)	Survey scientists, trade officials, and foreign standards organizations on creation/acceptance
Global nature of subject	Provide place for int'l collaboration or cooperation; enable sharing of data (e.g., NOAA's hurricane database)	Extent of usage of facility compared with use of a similar domestic facility; extent to which research conducted is published/cited; development of data used in published reports	Establish global standards that allow cooperative research or commerce; enable access to data to increase research efficiency (e.g., standard for common pollution monitoring equipment)	Survey scientists, trade officials, and foreign standards organizations on creation/acceptance
Unique foreign expertise	Build labs where expertise/subject of study is located to encourage cooperation and excellence (e.g., polar research labs in Antarctica)	Extent of publication compared with that of similar projects ($ per subject); citation counts of jointly authored papers vice U.S.-authored papers; cost of facility per unit of knowledge compared with similar or ideal facility	Gain access to unique foreign data that will enable U.S. research (USGS[a] access to Chilean seismology data set)	Survey scientists or agency officials; report on ability to access and share data, and on usefulness of data for research; publication counts
Government/ agency mission	Provide technical expertise to another country in need of improving national science for int'l benefit (e.g., CDC/USGS[a] work in Russia on mine safety)	Expert judgment of improvement of foreign science; reduce measurable hazards; increase in foreign nationals' publication of int'lly recognized work	Establish global standards that allow cooperative research or commerce; enable access to data to increase research efficiency (e.g., NIST project on silicon density measures)	Survey agency and/or cooperating partner on extent of national or global standards creation/acceptance

[a]U.S. Geological Survey.

to-scientist collaboration. NSF projects, however, tend to involve close collaboration among researchers. Each type of research and development activity, as well as the reasons for the research and the expected benefits, must be considered in crafting measures.

In addition to helping the program officer identify measures that might apply to a specific program, this framework may also be useful to the executive-level policymaker negotiating international agreements. By referring to the framework, the policymaker can identify measures that he or she may wish to "build in" to international agreements to help monitor how well projects under these agreements are meeting the goals laid out by the governments and cooperating parties.

A CASE STUDY ON EARTHQUAKES AND SEISMOLOGY

To test the ability of the framework approach to provide measures to track activities and provide feedback on benefits, RAND conducted a case study of international cooperative research and development in earthquake sciences and seismology. This subject was chosen because of the active nature of U.S. cooperation with other countries in this field, because of the growing importance of disaster preparedness and relief, and because activities in this area range from collaborative research projects, to technical support, to sharing data and equipment. In the process, RAND developed useful data about earthquake sciences and seismology, but the principal goal of this case study was to see if it is possible to use the framework to identify measures that provide feedback to policymakers on the benefits of ICRD.

Focusing on earthquake sciences and seismology, RAND used the RaDiUS inventory and other sources to first identify the full range of international cooperative activities being pursued by U.S. government-funded scientists. Second, we examined goals established at the interagency level for cooperative research and development activities. We analyzed these data to identify the type of cooperation being pursued, the countries involved, and the nature of the activities.

Based on the framework and RAND's review of the nature of the research, expected benefits and possible measures for this activity were identified. Expected benefits can be classified as access to subject of study, leveraging scarce funds, reducing global hazards, and access to foreign data and equipment that will allow research to proceed that might not otherwise have been possible. Based on what we viewed as workable measures, we decided to test three:

- *Bibliometrics:* A citation survey of papers authored jointly by U.S. and foreign researchers in 1985 and 1995 on the assumption that, since cooperative research has increased, jointly authored papers would increase.
- *Survey:* A participant survey, asking researchers to what extent foreign partners contributed resources, either financial or in-kind, to the project.

- *Expert judgment:* Experts reporting on the technology standards that dominate equipment used in joint research to determine the extent to which the United States is leading other countries in technology development.

Then, using this framework, we identified two reasons for ICRD cooperation: the global nature of the subject and the very large scale of equipment or nature of investment. Earthquakes and tremors occur every day all around the world. In a number of countries, seismographic equipment measures these faults and tremors and produces scientific data. Collection of this data analysis of trends provides the basis for international cooperation. In addition, large, expensive "shake tables" provide an experimental field to generate different types of earth shaking at varying intensities so that scientists can measure the effect of tremors on building structures. Japan and the United States have the two most advanced shake tables in the world. The two tables have complementary research capabilities and so are shared by researchers from both the United States and Japan as well as researchers from around the world.

Measures we identified as appropriate for collaborative research on global subjects and for large-scale research were considered. In this case study, we focused our inquiry on measuring the benefits of collaborative research and standards setting because these activities dominate U.S. government-funded ICRD in this area.

Bibliometrics

A citation survey conducted for this study used two scientific bibliographic services to identify papers on subjects that reflected one or more terms on a list developed for this part of the study. The research contained in these bibliographies was limited to basic research. The survey showed that papers jointly authored by a U.S. scientist and a foreign scientist rose to 585 papers in 1995 from 379 in 1985, even while funding remained constant in real terms. More joint papers were multinational in authorship in 1995 than in 1985. When papers were written by only two authors, Japanese researchers were the most likely collaborators, followed by Russian and Chinese, respectively. Data does not exist to compare the amount of R&D funds committed to earthquake sciences and seismology in 1985. Anecdotal reports from scientists indicate that total U.S. dollar funding for this research may have been higher in real terms in 1985, although ICRD may have claimed a smaller share of the funding than it did in 1995.

Survey

In a survey of one-fourth of the principal investigators associated with ICRD projects researching earthquakes or seismology, RAND found that, on average, the foreign financial contribution equals the U.S. contribution. In three-fourths of the projects surveyed, investigators reported either financial or in-kind contributions to the cooperative project. Of these projects reporting a foreign contribution, 47 percent had a foreign contribution that exceeded the U.S. contribution; 35 percent had an equal contribution from both sides; and 28 percent had a foreign contribution that was less

than the U.S. side. The highest leverage of funds was for research projects with Japan.

Expert Judgment: Standards

In an informal survey of experts on the standards that guide the development of seismology equipment, U.S. companies and research labs are setting the standard for 80 percent of the essential research equipment used in this field. In the area of building codes and local safety standards, while U.S. building and safety standards are often studied by foreign officials and researchers, the United States is not setting the world standard—in large part because building and safety codes are locally determined based on specific terrain and urban design. These standards are difficult to export to other parts of the world.

Qualitative Findings

During the course of the survey, researchers reported that, as a result of government funding and the existence of S&T agreements to encourage earthquake research, they had been able to establish excellent ongoing relationships with foreign scientists. During their research, U.S. scientists and engineers report meeting key foreign researchers, leading to opportunities to share data and conduct additional joint research. Joint papers often resulted from these activities. Moreover, both U.S. and foreign students were trained as a result of these projects. These activities have helped U.S. researchers stay at the state of the art in earthquake and seismological research, according to several researchers.

LESSONS LEARNED

The tools used and the data collected for this case study give a good picture of benefits accruing to the United States as a result of participation in ICRD. The case study did not succeed in identifying these benefits with existing data—new data collection through survey methods was required to get a full picture. Moreover, quantitative measures appear to be enriched by the qualitative reports received during the course of the survey, providing a fuller picture of the benefits of research.

One of the goals of this case study was to test whether unobtrusive methods are available to gather data on the benefits of ICRD. Indicators or output measures that are already collected or readily available would reduce the need for special studies to estimate how well ICRD is meeting goals and could provide a continual monitoring mechanism. Unobtrusive measures are important because, once investigators are asked to report on specific aspects of research, these factors tend to become the "goals" toward which researchers strive. This case study did not find that unobtrusive measures will provide a full picture of benefits, at least not at this time. A survey of principal investigators was necessary to identify the extent to which projects were leveraging foreign financial contributions. Additional data collection may help to reduce the extent to which direct surveys are required.

Chapter Five

CONCLUSION

International cooperation in research and development is an important activity to the U.S. government: Billions of dollars are spent on a rich and varied set of interactions every year. The nature of the activity—diverse locations, variety of topics, multiple goals—makes it difficult to track spending, assess the benefits, and ultimately defend the activity to Congress and the American public. Moreover, the disconnection between agreements signed at the executive level of government and the actual commitment of funds to collaborative research makes it difficult to know what the United States has promised to fund and what ICRD is actually being conducted. Finally, the dearth of well-developed measures for ongoing research complicates efforts to describe the benefits of these activities. This chapter discusses the positive and negative implications of this disconnection and briefly describes possible approaches to improving government's ability to track ICRD spending and assess benefits.

SCIENTIFIC OPPORTUNITY VERSUS POLITICAL EXPEDIENCY

The ability to describe the benefits of ICRD to the American public and its congressional representatives is particularly important given the opinion of some that international cooperation provides aid to foreigners at the expense of U.S. science, or that the interests of "good science" are subjugated to political interests. To test or refute this assertion, an effort must be made to describe actual, ongoing R&D activities and measure the benefits of these activities. The inventory of actual ICRD spending conducted for this study found a rich and varied amount of ICRD taking place across many agencies. Also, the case study suggests that the United States may be receiving significant benefits from this type of activity.

In the course of examining actual ICRD activities, we found little to support the idea that ICRD is primarily another form of "foreign aid." Quite the contrary, we learned that ICRD is primarily aimed at fulfilling the mission of the sponsoring agency, not to fulfill an international agreement. U.S. government agencies tend to guard their R&D funds jealously: Program managers do not spend dollars for the sake of political expediency. Given that most R&D spending decisions are made at the program level, and to the extent that ICRD is a part of that, this suggests that U.S. government funding for ICRD, on average (and perhaps better than average), is funding good science. Moreover, nothing in our research indicates that the interests of science and

the interests of politics are in conflict. Certainly, federal agencies conduct ICRD to achieve multiple agendas, among them, scientific opportunity, technical efficiency, and strategic benefit. ICRD serves all three goals:

- Government grant-making activity funds scientific researchers seeking to gain access to an important global or foreign scientific resource or to collaborate with a leading foreign researcher.
- Government improves technical efficiency by cooperating with other countries on projects in which each country produces a piece of a larger system and cooperates in its final production.
- The government works with other countries to contain nuclear waste, to reduce pollution, to alleviate suffering and the spread of infectious disease, in a way that serves strategic and political needs.

Some ICRD provides only indirect or long-term benefits to the U.S. taxpayer; even in these cases, cooperation enhances the U.S. science base by increasing scientific knowledge and access to resources and data. The case study on earthquake sciences and seismology examined a number of projects that had only indirect benefit to U.S. citizens. However, the United States is leveraging foreign research dollars and greatly increasing new knowledge created about earthquakes. This benefit will eventually accrue to citizens in enhanced disaster preparedness. Another example might be efforts by AID to contain infectious disease in Africa. U.S. citizens benefit only indirectly from this activity, but U.S. researchers learn a great deal about the etiology of infectious disease in ways that will benefit the United States.

Failure to follow through on ISTAs signed between the United States and other countries paradoxically provides evidence of the relative absence of conflict between scientific opportunity and political goals. If an agency does not see scientific advantage to cooperating with another country, that agency often does not follow through on an executive-level government-to-government agreement to fund research. Most agencies report that scientific or technological opportunity determines whether a project will be funded, not whether it is required by an international agreement. Many agencies report that an umbrella agreement to cooperate with another country in a specific area of science would play only a minor role in the decision to fund research.

Indeed, government officials report that agency-level agreements, rather than "umbrella" or framework agreements, often result from joint identification of an opportunity for mutual benefit. While these projects are not always implemented—research is risky, after all—agency-based agreements may be an indicator of scientific opportunity in many cases.

BRINGING ICRD WITHIN THE FOLD OF INTERNATIONAL SCIENCE AND TECHNOLOGY AGREEMENTS

While the government currently maintains hundreds of agreements to conduct ICRD, not all scientific cooperation takes place under a government-to-government

agreement. Some agencies keep careful track of what activities fall under which agreements, but not all agencies limit projects to those that have signed agreements. Moreover, contractors and grantees, being several steps removed from the government's diplomatic concerns, are sometimes unaware that they are working under a bilateral or multilateral S&T agreement. For cases in which intellectual property is created or trade or other disputes arise, ignorance about the regulations governing ownership, licensing, and royalties can have significant implications for where the intellectual property is commercialized. Moreover, for cases in which additional or new activities are being negotiated, it would be helpful to decisionmakers to have a map of where existing activities are occurring.

It may be useful to policymakers and agency officials to set a baseline to determine which R&D activities take place under ISTAs, and which take place outside them. Then, as agencies fund additional activities or sign new ISTAs, they could report this information on a Web page or other electronic repository. Given the advances in computer networking, this type of data collection should be relatively easy. These data would be very useful to U.S. and foreign researchers looking for opportunities to cooperate with others.

Continually refining our understanding of how best to measure ICRD will help to improve the efficiency and effectiveness of these activities. In addition, asking researchers and program managers how they would assess the effectiveness of ICRD activities would provide useful input to the process of collecting data and assessing progress.

IMPROVING DATA COLLECTION

To better track ICRD, link it to ISTAs, and measure benefits, improved data creation and tracking are needed. Data are available to assess the benefits of ICRD. Collected efficiently, placed in proper context, and combined with qualitative testimony, these data can provide usable information to help decisionmakers track benefits and compare the returns on one activity against others. The framework suggested in this report provides a way to select measures and organize the data to streamline the assessment of and perhaps ultimately defend international R&D cooperation.

Improved data, provided in a timely way, would greatly enhance the ability of program managers and policymakers to monitor ICRD. The relevance and availability of the measures suggested in this study should be improved and additional ones should be developed. In the process, priority should be given to less intrusive measures, such as bibliometric publication and citation data and milestones, so that measurement does not unduly influence the choices researchers make when conducting ICRD projects. Given that these unobtrusive measures are scarce, additional research and development is needed to refine indicators and to suggest the best methods for collecting and aggregating measures.

Program managers and policymakers may wish to work at the agency level to develop a system of "signposts" that report on outputs and that track the relevance of those outputs to the scientific and technical community. This could include periodic re-

ports on the excellence of ICRD taking place in a particular field. Bibliometric tools can count the number of jointly authored publications relative to U.S.-authored papers and the relative frequency of citations of jointly authored publications. Government agencies such as the DoC National Technical Information Service and government contractors such as Scientific Citations, Inc. could be tasked to refine measures of the outputs of ICRD, to craft signposts of progress, and to make these data more consistently available to government offices.

Two additional actions could improve ICRD data and, thereby, government monitoring. First, agencies should add a request for measures to international project plans. Many agencies are already developing these measures and collecting these data in response to GPRA and other government accountability practices, but the measures collected at the agency level will not aggregate to the interagency level. A request to periodically provide these measures to the NSTC could help to create the data for interagency comparisons. Second, periodic review or continual data monitoring of international science and technology agreements should be requested. This data can be collected by the agencies, or by a technical agency such as the National Technical Information Service. The data can be aggregated at the NSTC level to provide feedback on the extent to which ISTAs are reaching their stated goals.

IMPROVING DATA ON SPENDING

Information about the benefits of ICRD accruing to the United States would provide input to agency and NSTC-level funding decisions. However, a method needs to be developed to track ICRD spending over time. This study examined only one fiscal year, 1995, of government ICRD spending, and the data collection and analysis process were labor intensive. Providing a monitoring capability of ICRD year-to-year would require one of the following:

- The easiest approach would be to collect yearly R&D data on ICRD-intensive programs. Analysts would be able to take a percentage of spending (say 4.5 percent, to track with RAND's finding of ICRD's 4.5 percent of all R&D spending) as representative of ICRD spending. The summary table in Appendix A contains a list of relevant bureaus. The outlines in Appendix B list the relevant programs. Such an approach would provide an approximate figure of ICRD activities, but it may miss significant changes and subtle shifts that take place from year to year. Moreover, it would not allow the cross-agency comparisons that provide input to the assessment framework.
- A second option would be to reproduce every few years a cross-cutting inventory like this one. This approach would provide useful snapshots of activities and a trend analysis, but it would not provide data to allow decisionmakers to track activity and make key interventions in programs that are showing significant promise or are lagging expectations.
- A third and more time-consuming, but ultimately more comprehensive, approach would be to ask agencies to "tag" ICRD activities for the purposes of budgeting and reporting. This would allow tracking over time, would show trends,

and would allow analysts, program managers, and policymakers to aggregate the data for the purposes of cross-cutting analysis. A tagging system could also provide a way for agencies to identify which activities take place under international science and technology agreements, and within this category, which of these activities may produce scientific results or intellectual property of commercial value.

Appendix A

BREAKDOWN OF AGENCY SUPPORT FOR ICRD

Table A.1

Breakdown of Agency Support for ICRD

Agency	Bureaus Supporting ICRD	FY95 R&D Budget (K) Total and By Bureau	ICRD Spending on Awards as Identified by RAND (K)	Statutory Authority to Engage in Int'l Cooperation	Number of Int.l Sci & Tech Bilateral Agrts Reported Title V	Number of Int.l Sci & Tech Agrts Reported to RAND	Use (Circ-175) State Dep. Approval Process	Number of Inventions Resulting from ICRD
GRAND TOTALS		**$ 63,986,000**	**$ 3,129,614**		**585**			**64**
Agriculture		**$ 1,375,000**	**$ 7,525**		**30**		**Yes**	**3**
	Agriculture Research Service	$ 666,000	$ 9					
	Animal and Plant Health Inspection Service	$ 19,000	$ 10					
	Cooperative State Research, Education and Extension Service	$ 419,000	$ 2,485					
	Foreign Agricultural Service	$ 1,400	$ 1,784					
	Forest Service	$ 200,000	$ 3,237					
Commerce	**TOTAL**	**$ 1,183,000**	**$ 4,167**		**86**	**not reported**	**Yes**	**33**
	Main			22 USC 2656d (a)	1	not reported	Yes	7
	National Oceanic & Atmospheric Administration	$ 549,300	$ 3,167	15 USC Sec. 2901, 16 USC Sec. 1801, 49 USC Sec. 1463, 33 USC 1121, 33 USC Sec. 833	53	not reported	Yes	0
	Census	$ 5,400	$ -		3	not reported	Yes	0

Table A.1—continued

Agency	Bureaus Supporting ICRD	FY95 R&D Budget (K) Total and By Bureau	ICRD Spending on Awards as Identified by RAND (K)	Statutory Authority to Engage in Int'l Cooperation	Number of Int.l Sci & Tech Bilateral Agrts Reported Title V	Number of Int.l Sci & Tech Agrts Reported to RAND	Use (Circ-175) State Dep. Approval Process	Number of Inventions Resulting from ICRD
	NIST	$ 623,000	$ 1,000	15 USC 273 and 278(g)	23	not reported	Yes	26
	NTIA	$ 4,600	$ -		5	5	Yes	0
Defense	**TOTAL**	**$ 36,335,000**	**$ 465,196**	**22 USC 2767, 10 USC 2350A-a1, 10 USC 3013**	**53**	**not reported**	**No**	**12**
	Advanced Research Project Technical Support	$ 2,732,000	$ 71,068					
	Ballistic Missile Defense Organization	$ 2,468,000	$ 42,059					
	Defense Nuclear Agency	$ 255,000	$ 5,479					
	OSD	$ 1,923,000	$ 1,030	22 USC 2767, 10 USC 2350A-a1, 10 USC 3013	17	not reported	No	0
	Air Force	$ 12,057,000	$ 98,566	22 USC 2767, 10 USC 2350A-a1, 10 USC 3013	10	not reported	No	0
	Army	$ 5,481,000	$ 243,057	22 USC 2767, 10 USC 2350A-a1, 10 USC 3013	7	109	No	6
	Navy	$ 8,695,000	$ 3,936	22 USC 2767, 10 USC 2350A-a1, 10 USC 3013	19	not reported	No	6
	Defense Environmental Restoration and Waste Management	$ 215,000	$ 1,278					
	Energy conservation	$ 390,000	$ 1,934					
	Energy Supply	$ 1,963,000	$ 10,547					
	Fossil Energy	$ 383,000	$ 142					

Table A.1—continued

Agency	Bureaus Supporting ICRD	FY95 R&D Budget (K) Total and By Bureau	ICRD Spending on Awards as Identified by RAND (K)	Statutory Authority to Engage in Int'l Cooperation	Number of Int.l Sci & Tech Bilateral Agrts Reported Title V	Number of Int.l Sci & Tech Agrts Reported to RAND	Use (Circ-175) State Dep. Approval Process	Number of Inventions Resulting from ICRD
	General Science and Research Activities	$ 700,100	$ 21,580					
	LDRD (Lab directed Research and Development)		$ 190					
	Materials Support and Other Defense Programs	$ 880,000	$ 200					
	Uranium Enrichment	$ 2,500	$ 4,236					
	WFO (Work for Others)		$ 2,738					
	Labs		$ 128,633					
EPA		**$ 584,000**	**$ 26,117**		**24**	**not reported**	**Yes**	**1**
	Research and Development	$ 349,000	$ 26,117					
Health and Human Services	**TOTAL**	**$ 11,412,000**	**$ 122,547**		**61**	**not reported**		**9**
	CDC	$ 225,350	$ 14,303			10		0
	FDA	$ 188,000						0
	NIH	$ 10,698,000	$ 105,602			84		9
	Agency for Health Care Policy and Research	$ 139,000	$ 2,642					
Interior		**$ 681,000**	**$ 384**	**43 USC 31b, 43 USC 7701**	**102**	**56**	**Yes**	**0**
	USGS		$ 384					
NASA		**$ 9,078,000**	**$ 1,939,785**	**42 USC 2540 Sec. 205**	**60**		**Yes**	**0**

Table A.1— continued

Agency	Bureaus Supporting ICRD	FY95 R&D Budget (K) Total and By Bureau	ICRD Spending on Awards as Identified by RAND (K)	Statutory Authority to Engage in Int'l Cooperation	Number of Int.l Sci & Tech Bilateral Agrts Reported Title V	Number of Int.l Sci & Tech Agrts Reported to RAND	Use (Circ-175) State Dep. Approval Process	Number of Inventions Resulting from ICRD
	Aeronautical Research and Technology	$ 1,204,000	$ 837					
	Mission to Planet Earth	$ 1,394,000	$ 782,121					
	Space Access & Technology	$ 783,000	$ 222					
	Space Science	$ 1,986,000	$ 576,915					
	Space Shuttle		$ 79,500					
	Space Station	$ 2,026,000	$ 467,471					
National Science Foundation		**$ 2,145,000**	**$ 220,780**	**42 USC 1862, 42 USC 1870, 42 USC 1872,**	**15**		Yes	6
	Biological Sciences (BIO)	$ 301,000	$ 12,759					
	Computer & Information Science & Engineering (CSE)	$ 231,000	$ 2,246					
	Education & Human Resources (EHR)	$ 107,000	$ 2,851					
	Engineering (ENG)	$ 320,000	$ 6,137					
	Geosciences (GEO)	$ 403,000	$ 28,451					
	Mathematical & Physical Sciences (MPS)	$ 629,000	$ 16,686					
	National Astronomy & Ionospheric Center		$ 7,820					
	National Center for Atmospheric Research		$ 58,380					

Table A.1— continued

Agency	Bureaus Supporting ICRD	FY95 R&D Budget (K) Total and By Bureau	ICRD Spending on Awards as Identified by RAND (K)	Statutory Authority to Engage in Int'l Cooperation	Number of Int.l Sci & Tech Bilateral Agrts Reported Title V	Number of Int.l Sci & Tech Agrts Reported to RAND	Use (Circ-175) State Dep. Approval Process	Number of Inventions Resulting from ICRD
	National Optical Astronomy Observatories		$ 26,690					
	National Radio Astronomy Observatory		$ 28,870					
	Social, Behavioral & Economic Sciences (SBE)	$ 100,000	$ 22,682					
	U.S. Polar Research programs (DPP, OPP)	$ 55,000	$ 7,209					
Nuclear Regulatory Commission		**$ 86,000**	**$ 12**	**Atomic Energy Act**	**73**	**60**	**Yes**	**0**
	Reactor Safety Research	$ 71,000	$ 12					
Smithsonian		**$ 132,000**	**$ 29,150**		**1**	**2**	**No**	**0**
	Arts & Humanities Programs (S&E Account)	$ 19,000	$ 600					
	Canal Zone Biological Area fund (Sep. from S&E Account)	$ 150	$ 150					
	Other Programs (S&E Account)	$ 51,000	$ 354					
	Science Programs	$ 63,000	$ 28,043					
State	**AID**	**$ 314,000**	**$ 313,951**	**1 USC 112b, 22 USC 256d**	**52**		**Yes**	**0**

Table A.1— continued

Agency	Bureaus Supporting ICRD	FY95 R&D Budget (K) Total and By Bureau	ICRD Spending on Awards as Identified by RAND (K)	Statutory Authority to Engage in Int'l Cooperation	Number of Int.l Sci & Tech Bilateral Agrts Reported Title V	Number of Int.l Sci & Tech Agrts Reported to RAND	Use (Circ-175) State Dep. Approval Process	Number of Inventions Resulting from ICRD
	Africa	$ 73,000	$ 73,343					
	Asia/Near East	$ 26,000	$ 25,528					
	Europe & Newly Independent States	$ 22,500	$ 22,500					
	Global	$ 162,000	$ 162,049					
	Latin America & Caribbean	$ 21,000	$ 20,758					
	Policy, Program. and Coordination	$ 9,800	$ 9,773					
Transportation		**$ 661,000**	**$ -**	**49 USC 301**	**28**	**not reported**	Yes	0

Appendix B

OUTLINE OF GOVERNMENT PROGRAMS REPORTING INTERNATIONAL COOPERATION IN RESEARCH AND DEVELOPMENT (FROM RaDiUS)

Federal Organizations Active in Specified Area - Outline

RaDiUS™

Main Query Screen	Save Current Query	Glossary of Terms	RaDiUS Information	Help	Show Query Criteria
Query Summary	View by Fed Org	View by Award/Task	Download		

Query Specifications:

Fiscal Year: 1995
Federal Organization(s): All Federal Organizations
Search term(s): (('russia') or ('australia') or ('japan') or ('canada') or ('united kingdom') or ('germany') or ('israel') or ('china') or ('mexico') or ('india') or ('france') or ('brazil') or ('taiwan') or ('thailand') or ('costa rica') or ('italy') or ('venezuela') or ('european union') or ('africa') or ('central america') or ('south america') or ('asia')) and (not 'hamster')
Performer(s): All performers
Level 5 Award criteria: All awards

Overview of Query Results:

Note: A more detailed report including budget authority and obligation information for all Federal Organizations involved in the specified activity/area is also available.

- Level 1 **Agency for International Development**
  - Level 2 Africa
  - Level 2 Asia/Near East
  - Level 2 Global
    - Level 3 Agriculture
    - Level 3 Ctr for University Cooperation in Development

- Level 1 **Department of Agriculture**
  - Level 2 Agricultural Marketing Service
  - Level 2 Agriculture Research Service
    - Level 3 Extramural awards
    - Level 3 Research on animal sciences
      - Level 4 BARC/Livestock and Poultry Science Institute (MD/Beltsville)
      - Level 4 Medical and Veterinary Entomology Research Laboratory (FL/Gainesville)+
      - Level 4 Screwworm Research Laboratory (Mexico/Tuxla Gutierrez)
    - Level 3 Research on commodity, conversion, and delivery
      - Level 4 Food Animal Protection Research Laboratory (TX/College Station)+
      - Level 4 Red River Valley Agricutural Research Center (ND/Fargo)+
    - Level 3 Research on plant sciences
      - Level 4 Aquatic Weed Control Research Laboratory (FL/Fort Lauderdale)
      - Level 4 Aquatic Weeds Control Research Laboratory (CA/Davis)
      - Level 4 BARC/Plant Sciences Institute (MD/Beltsville)
      - Level 4 Crop Protection Research Laboratory (IL/Urbana)
      - Level 4 European Biocontrol Research Laboratory (France/Montpelier)
      - Level 4 Foreign Disease - Weed Science Research Laboratory (MD/Frederick)
      - Level 4 Fruit and Vegetable Insect Research Laboratory (WA/Yakima)
      - Level 4 Honey Bee Breeding, Genetics, & Physiology Research Laboratory (LA/Baton Rouge)
      - Level 4 Plant Physiology and Genetics Research Laboratory (IL/URbana)

- Level 4 Range Weeds and Cereals Research Laboratory (MT/Bozeman)
- Level 4 Southern Crops Research Laboratory (TX/College Station)
- Level 4 Soybean and Nitrogen Fixation Research Laboratory (NC/Raleigh)
- Level 4 U.S. Horticultural Research Laboratory (FL/Orlando)
- Level 4 U.S. National Arboretum (DC)
- Level 3 Research on soil, water, and air sciences
- Level 4 Natural Resources Research Center (CO/Fort Collins)+
- Level 4 Southwest Watershed Research Center (AZ/Tucson)
- Level 2 Animal & Plant Health Inspection Service
- Level 3 Extramural awards
- Level 2 Cooperative State Research, Education & Extension Service
- Level 3 Animal health & disease research
- Level 4 MN - Minnesota
- Level 4 NM - New Mexico
- Level 3 McIntire-Stennis cooperative forestry
- Level 4 CT - Connecticut
- Level 4 ME - Maine
- Level 4 NC - North Carolina
- Level 4 NH - New Hampshire
- Level 4 NM - New Mexico
- Level 4 NY - New York
- Level 3 National research initiative
- Level 4 Extramural awards
- Level 3 Payments to 1890 colleges & Tuskegee (Evans-Allen)
- Level 4 MD - Maryland
- Level 3 Payments under the Hatch Act
- Level 4 AL - Alabama
- Level 4 AZ - Arizona
- Level 4 CA - California
- Level 4 CO - Colorado
- Level 4 FL - Florida
- Level 4 HI - Hawaii
- Level 4 IA - Iowa
- Level 4 ID - Idaho
- Level 4 IN - Indiana
- Level 4 KS - Kansas
- Level 4 MI - Michigan
- Level 4 MN - Minnesota
- Level 4 MO - Missouri
- Level 4 NE - Nebraska
- Level 4 NM - New Mexico
- Level 4 NY - New York
- Level 4 OR - Oregon
- Level 4 PA - Pennsylvania
- Level 4 SD - South Dakota
- Level 4 TX - Texas
- Level 4 UT - Utah

- Level 4 VA - Virginia
- Level 4 VT - Vermont
- Level 4 WA - Washington
- Level 4 WI - Wisconsin
- Level 4 WY - Wyoming
- Level 3 Special research grants
- Level 3 [Small business innovative research]
- Level 2 Foreign Agricultural Service
- Level 2 Forest Service
- Level 3 Extramural awards
- Level 3 Forest environment research
- Level 3 Forest management research
- Level 3 Resource analyses research

Level 1 **Department of Commerce**

- Level 2 Economic Development Administration
- Level 2 National Institute of Standards & Technology
- Level 3 Building and Fire Research Laboratory
- Level 3 Chemical Science and Technology Laboratory
- Level 4 Biotechnology
- Level 3 Electronics and Electrical Engineering Laboratory
- Level 4 Semiconductor electronics
- Level 3 Extramural awards for measurement & engineering research & standards
- Level 3 Industrial technology services
- Level 4 Advanced Technology Program
- Level 3 Materials Science and Engineering Laboratory
- Level 4 Materials Science and Engineering Laboratory Office
- Level 2 National Oceanic & Atmospheric Administration
- Level 3 National Environmental Satellite, Data, and Information Service
- Level 4 Environmental data management systems
- Level 4 Satellite observing systems
- Level 3 National Marine Fisheries Service
- Level 4 Fisheries development program
- Level 4 Information collection & analyses
- Level 3 Oceanic and Atmospheric Research
- Level 4 Atmospheric programs
- Level 4 Climate and air quality control
- Level 4 Ocean and great lakes programs
- Level 4 Office of the Assistant Administrator
- Level 3 Office of the Administrator, including program support

Level 1 **Department of Defense**

- Level 2 Ballistic Missile Defense Organization
- Level 3 0603173C - Support Technologies/Follow-on Technologies - Adv Tech Dev
- Level 4 1155 - Phenomenology Program
- Level 4 2259 - ACES/ADP
- Level 4 Project number unspecified
- Level 3 0603215C - Limited Defense System

- Level 4 Project number unspecified
- Level 3 0603216C - Theater Missile Defenses
  - Level 4 1106 - Sens Stud & Exp
  - Level 4 1206 - Advanced Tmd Weapons
  - Level 4 2104T - GROUND-BASED RADAR
  - Level 4 2209 - ARROW/ACES
  - Level 4 3201 - Architecture & Studies
  - Level 4 3300 - Test & Eval Support
  - Level 4 Project number unspecified
- Level 3 0603217C - Ballistic Missile Defense Tech
  - Level 4 1106 - Sens Stud & Exp
  - Level 4 1209 - Endo Tech
  - Level 4 1307 - DEW Demo
  - Level 4 2104 - GBR
  - Level 4 3201 - Architecture & Studies
  - Level 4 3300 - Test & Eval Support
- Level 3 0603218C - Research and Support Activities
  - Level 4 3300 - Test & Eval Support
  - Level 4 Project number unspecified
- Level 3 0603861C - Theater High-Altitude Area Defense System - TMD - Dem/Val
  - Level 4 2260 - THAAD
- Level 3 0603869C - CORPS Surface-to-Air Missile - TMD - Dem/Val
  - Level 4 1262 - Corps Sam
- Level 3 0603871C - National Missile Defense - Dem/Val
  - Level 4 1151 - Sensors (Active and Passive)
  - Level 4 1155 - Phenomenology Program
- Level 3 0603872C - Other Theater Missile Defense/Follow-on TMD Act Acq - Dem/Val
  - Level 4 1294 - UAV Boost Phase Intercept
  - Level 4 2259 - ACES/ADP
- Level 3 0604216C - Theater Missile Defense (Dem/Val)
  - Level 4 2104 - GBR
  - Level 4 2207 - Patriot
  - Level 4 2208 - ERINT
  - Level 4 2213 - Sea Based TMD Int
  - Level 4 3300 - Test & Eval Support
- Level 3 0604225C - Theater Missile Defense Acquisition EMD Programs
  - Level 4 2104 - 0604225C RDT&E Theater Missile Defense Ground Based Radar (TMD-GBR)
  - Level 4 2207 - 0604225C RDT&E PATRIOT ONLY
  - Level 4 2213 - 0604225C RDT&E Sea-based Theater Missile Defense capablity

- Level 2 CRADAs - Defense Agencies
- Level 2 Chemical & Biological Defense Program
  - Level 3 0604384BP - Chemical & Biological Defense Program
    - Level 4 BJ5 - Biological Defense
- Level 2 Defense Advanced Research Projects Agency
  - Level 3 0601101E - Defense Research Sciences
    - Level 4 Project number unspecified
  - Level 3 0602301E - Computing Systems & Communications Tech

- Level4 Project number unspecified
- Level4 ST-23 - Counter Proliferation Technology
- Level3 0602702E - Tactical Technology
- Level4 Project number unspecified
- Level3 0602712E - Materials & Electronics Technology
- Level4 Project number unspecified
- Level3 0603226E - Experimntl Eval. of Major Innovative Tech
- Level4 EE-24 - ASTOVL/CTOL
- Level4 EE-27 - Advanced Space Technology Program
- Level3 0603569E - Advanced Submarine Technology
- Level4 AS-01 - SUBTECH
- Level3 0603570E - Defense Reinvestment
- Level4 P-520 - Defense Reinvestment
- Level3 0603739E - Advanced Electronics Technologies
- Level4 MT-07 - Centers of Excellence
- Level4 Project number unspecified
- Level2 Defense Information Systems Agency
- Level3 0302019K - Jt/Defense Info Systems Engineering & Integration
- Level4 T65 - Cincusacom Support
- Level4 T66 - CINC/JTF C4 Integration
- Level3 0303126K - Long-Haul Communications (DCS)
- Level4 U50 - Defense Switched Network (DSN)/Defense Information System (DIS) Technology Insertion (TI)
- Level2 Defense Investigative Service
- Level2 Defense Nuclear Agency
- Level3 0602715H - Defense Nuclear Agency
- Level4 AC - Weapon Systems Lethality
- Level4 AD - Biomedical/Lifesciences
- Level4 AF - Weapon Systems Operability
- Level4 Project number unspecified
- Level3 0603711H - Verification Technology Demo
- Level4 CC - Chemical Weapons Convention Technology
- Level4 CD - Yield Measurement Technology
- Level4 CE - Cooperative Threat Reduction
- Level2 Department of the Air Force
- Level3 0101113F - B-52 Squadrons
- Level4 4258 - Have Lite Study
- Level3 0102325F - Joint Surveillance System
- Level4 2976 - Joint Surveillance System (JSS) Connectivity
- Level3 0102411F - North Atlantic Defense System
- Level4 3159 - CARIBBEAN BASIN RADAR NETWORK (CBRN)
- Level3 0102412F - North Warning Systems (NWS)
- Level4 2710 - North Warning System (NWS)
- Level3 0207129F - F-111 Squadrons
- Level4 1332 - F-111 Crew Escape Module Parachute Replacement
- Level3 0207133F - F-16 Squadrons
- Level4 2671 - F-16 Squadrons

- Level 3 0207411F - Overseas Air Weapon Control System
  - Level 4 2704 - EIFEL
- Level 3 0207417F - Airborne Warning and Control System (AWACS)
  - Level 4 411L - Airborne Warning & Control System
- Level 3 0303110F - Defense Satellite Communications System (SPACE)
  - Level 4 2638 - DSCS
- Level 3 0305164F - NAVSTAR Global Positioning System (USER Equip) (SPACE)
  - Level 4 3028 - Navstar Global Positioning System User Equipment
- Level 3 0305182F - Eastern Space Launch Facility (ESLF) (SPACE)
  - Level 4 4137 - Range Standardization and Automation (RSA)
- Level 3 0305909F - Ballistic Missile Early Warning System (BMEWS)
  - Level 4 2622 - Ballistic Missile Early Warning System (BMEWS)
- Level 3 0601101F - In-House Laboratory Independent Res
  - Level 4 Project number unspecified
- Level 3 0601102F - Defense Research Sciences
  - Level 4 2301 - Physics
  - Level 4 2308 - Propulsion
  - Level 4 2309 - Terrestrial Sciences
  - Level 4 2310 - Atmospheric Sciences
  - Level 4 2311 - Space Sciences
  - Level 4 2312 - Biological Sciences
  - Level 4 2313 - Human Performance
  - Level 4 4113 - Science and Engineering Education Programs
  - Level 4 Project number unspecified
- Level 3 0602101F - Geophysics
  - Level 4 4643 - IONOSPHERIC SPECIFICATION
  - Level 4 7659 - AEROSPACE SYSTEMS TECHNOLOGY
- Level 3 0602102F - Materials
  - Level 4 2423 - Electromagnetic Windows and Electronic Materials
- Level 3 0602201F - Aerospace Flight Dynamics
  - Level 4 2402 - Vehicle Equipment
  - Level 4 2403 - Flight Control
  - Level 4 2404 - Aeromechanics
  - Level 4 Project number unspecified
- Level 3 0602202F - Armstrong Lab Exploratory Development
  - Level 4 1123 - Manpower, Personnel, and Training Technology
  - Level 4 7184 - Human System Interface Technologies
  - Level 4 7755 - Aircrew Selection and Standards
  - Level 4 7757 - Radiation Hazards in Aerospace Operations
- Level 3 0602204F - Aerospace Avionics
  - Level 4 2000 - Active Electronic Countermeasures
  - Level 4 2001 - Electro-Optical Technology
  - Level 4 2004 - Reconnaissance/Strike Electro-Optical Sensors
- Level 3 0602206F - Civil Engineering & Environmental Quality
  - Level 4 2673 - Air Base Operability Technology
- Level 3 0602302F - Rocket Propulsion & Astronautics Tech
  - Level 4 Project number unspecified

- Level 3 0602601F - Phillips Lab Exploratory Development
    - Level 4 5797 - Advanced Weapons Technology and Assessments
    - Level 4 8809 - Satellite Technology
    - Level 4 Project number unspecified
- Level 3 0602602F - Conventional Munitions
    - Level 4 2502 - Ordnance Technology
- Level 3 0602702F - Command, Control & Communications
    - Level 4 4600 - Electromagnetic Technology
- Level 3 0603112F - Advanced Materials for Weapons Systems
    - Level 4 3153 - Non-Destructive Inspection Development
- Level 3 0603211F - Aerospace Structures
    - Level 4 69CW - Advanced Composites
- Level 3 0603245F - Flight Vehicle Technology Integration
    - Level 4 2568 - Air Vehicle Technology Integration
- Level 3 0603253F - Advanced Avionics Integration
    - Level 4 2733 - Advanced Reconnaissance/Strike Radars
- Level 3 0603401F - Advanced Spacecraft Technology
    - Level 4 3784 - Space Sensors and Satellite Communication Technology
    - Level 4 682J - Space Power and Thermal Management Technology
- Level 3 0603410F - Space Systems Environ Interaction Tech
    - Level 4 2822 - Space Environmental Impact Tests
- Level 3 0603605F - Advanced Radiation Technology
    - Level 4 3151 - High Power Semiconductor Laser Technology
    - Level 4 3152 - High Power Microwave (HPM) Technology
- Level 3 0603723F - Environmental Engineering Tech
    - Level 4 2104 - Air Base Operability Advanced Technology
    - Level 4 3037 - Noise and Sonic Boom Impact Technology
- Level 3 0603790F - NATO research & Development (H)
- Level 3 0603800F - Joint Advanced Strike Technology - Dem/Val
- Level 3 0604212F - Aircraft Equipment Development
    - Level 4 1926 - AIRCRAFT WINDSHIELD DEVELOPMENT
- Level 3 0604222F - Nuclear Weapons Support
    - Level 4 5708 - Nuclear Weapons Support
- Level 3 0604233F - Specialized Undergraduate Pilot Training
    - Level 4 4228 - T-3A Enhanced Flight Screener (EFS)
- Level 3 0604268F - Aircraft Engine Component Improvement Program
    - Level 4 Aircraft Engine Component Improvement Program (CIP)
- Level 3 0604708F - Civil, Fire, Environmental, Shelter Engineering
    - Level 4 2674 - Tactical Shelters
- Level 3 0604727F - Joint Standoff Weapons Systems
    - Level 4 1000 - Joint Standoff Weapons (JSOW)
- Level 3 0605502F - Small Business Innovative Research (H)
    - Level 4 Project number unspecified
- Level 3 0605708F - Navigation/Radar/Sled Track Test Support
    - Level 4 688G - Aircraft Navigation System Verification
- Level 3 0605807F - Test and Evaluation Support
    - Level 4 Project number unspecified

Level2 Department of the Army
- Level3 0203735A - Combat Vehicle Improvement Programs
  - Level4 D280 - Recovery Vehicle Improvement Program (IRV)
- Level3 0203740A - Maneuver Control System
  - Level4 D484 - Maneuver Control System
- Level3 0203801A - Missile/Air Defense Product Improvement Program
  - Level4 D036 - PATRIOT Product Improvement Program
  - Level4 D303 - STINGER-RMP Product Improvement Program
- Level3 0203802A - Other Missile Product Improvement Programs
  - Level4 D304 - Army TACMS Pre-planned Product Improvement Program
- Level3 0208051A - Joint Biological Defense Program
  - Level4 DBD1 - Joint biological Defense - Non-Medical
  - Level4 DBD2 - Joint Biological Defense-Medical
- Level3 0303142A - SATCOM Ground Environment
  - Level4 D253 - Defense Satellite Communications System-Defense Communications System (DSCS-DCS)(PHASE II)
- Level3 0601101A - In-House Laboratory Independent Research
  - Level4 A91C - In-House Laboratory Independent Research - Medical Research and Development Command
- Level3 0601102A - Defense Research Sciences
  - Level4 A305 - Automatic Target Recognition Research
  - Level4 A31B - Night Vision and Electro-Optics Research
  - Level4 A71A - Research in Chemical Warfare/Biological Warfare Defense
  - Level4 A751 - Department of Defense Dependent Schools
  - Level4 AF20 - Research in Vehicle Propulsion
  - Level4 AF22 - Research in Vehicular Mobility
  - Level4 AH40 - Signals Warfare Laboratory
  - Level4 AH42 - Materials and Mechanics
  - Level4 AH43 - Research in Ballistics
  - Level4 AH44 - Sensor Systems Research
  - Level4 AH45 - Air Mobility
  - Level4 AH47 - Electronic Device Research
  - Level4 AH48 - Communications Research
  - Level4 AH49 - Research in Missiles and High-Energy Lasers
  - Level4 AH51 - Combat Support
  - Level4 AH52 - Equipment for the Soldier
  - Level4 AH60 - Research in Armaments
  - Level4 AH61 - Research in Close Combat Weaponry
  - Level4 AH66 - Aviation Structures Research
  - Level4 AH68 - Processes in Pollution Abatement Technology
  - Level4 AT22 - Soil and Rock Mechanics
  - Level4 AT23 - Basic Research/Military Construction
  - Level4 AT24 - Snow, Ice and Frozen Soil
  - Level4 B52C - Mapping and Remote Sensing
  - Level4 B53A - Atmospheric Sciences
  - Level4 B74A - Human Engineering
  - Level4 B74F - Personnel Performance and Training
  - Level4 BH27 - Research in Munitions Science

- Level 4 BH57 - Scientific Problems with Military Applications
- Level 4 BH67 - Environmental Research - Army Materiel Command
- Level 4 BS04 - Military Pollutants and Health Hazards
- Level 4 BS11 - Science Base/Medical Chemical Defense
- Level 4 BS12 - Science Base/Medical Biological Defense
- Level 4 BS13 - Science Base/Medical Research Infectious Disease
- Level 4 BS14 - Science Base/Combat Casualty Care Research
- Level 4 BS15 - Science Base/System Health Hazards Research
- Level 4 BS16 - Science Base/Combat Dentistry Research
- Level 4 BS17 - Molecular Biology/Military HIV Research
- Level 4 BT25 - Environmental Research - Corps of Engineers
- Level 4 DH41 - NEUROSCIENCE CENTER

Level 3 0602105A - Materials Technology
- Level 4 AH84 - Materials

Level 3 0602120A - Sensors & Electronic Survivability
- Level 4 A140 - High Power Microwave (HPM) Technology
- Level 4 AH15 - Ground Combat Identification (ID) Technology
- Level 4 AH16 - Sensors, Signatures, Signal and Information Processing (S3I) Technology
- Level 4 AH25 - Nuclear Effects Survivability Technology

Level 3 0602270A - EW Technology
- Level 4 A442 - Tactical Electronic Warfare Technology
- Level 4 A906 - Tactical Electronic Warfare Techniques

Level 3 0602303A - Missile Technology
- Level 4 A214 - Missile Technology
- Level 4 DC04 - Smart Munition Technology Management

Level 3 0602618A - Ballistics Technology
- Level 4 AH80 - Ballistics Technology
- Level 4 AH81 - Armor/Anti-Armor MOU

Level 3 0602622A - Chemical, Smoke & Equip Defeating Tech.
- Level 4 A551 - NUCLEAR BIOLOGICAL CHEMICAL SURVIVABILITY
- Level 4 A552 - Smoke/Novel Effects Munitions
- Level 4 A553 - Chemical/Biological (CB) Defense & General Investigations

Level 3 0602709A - Night Vision Technology
- Level 4 DH95 - Night Vision and Electro-Optic Technology

Level 3 0602716A - Human Factors Engineering Technology
- Level 4 AH70 - Human Factors Engineering Systems Development

Level 3 0602720A - Environmental Quality Technology
- Level 4 A896 - Base Facility Environmental Quality

Level 3 0602782A - Command, Control, Communications Tech
- Level 4 A779 - Command/Control (C2) and Platform Integration Technology
- Level 4 AH92 - Communications Technology
- Level 4 AH93 - Combat Surveillance and Target Acquisition (CSTA) Technology

Level 3 0602784A - Military Engineering Technology
- Level 4 AH71 - Atmospheric Investigations
- Level 4 AT40 - Mobility & Weapons Effects Technology
- Level 4 AT42 - Cold Regions Engineering Technology

Level 3 0602785A - Manpower/Personnel/Training Technology

- Level 4 A790 - Personnel Systems and Performance Technology
- Level 4 A791 - Education and Training Technology
- Level 4 ABB2 - Life Science Technology

Level 3 0602786A - Logistics Technology
- Level 4 AH98 - Clothing & Equipment Technology
- Level 4 AH99 - Joint Services Food/System Technology
- Level 4 D283 - Airdrop Advanced Technology

Level 3 0602787A - Medical Technology
- Level 4 A870 - DoD Medical Defense Against Infectious Diseases
- Level 4 A873 - HIV Exploratory Research
- Level 4 A878 - Health Hazards of Military Materiel
- Level 4 A879 - Medical Factors Enhancing Soldier Effectiveness
- Level 4 A882 - Environmental Medical Unit
- Level 4 D873 - HIV Exploratory Research

Level 3 0603001A - Logistics Advanced Technology
- Level 4 D150 - Fuels and Lubricants
- Level 4 D242 - Airdrop Equipment
- Level 4 D528 - Acousto-Optic Tunable Filter (AOTF) Technology Demonstration
- Level 4 D543 - Ammunition Logistics
- Level 4 D544 - Cooperative Explosive Safety
- Level 4 D594 - Metrology and Calibration
- Level 4 DC07 - Joint Service Food Technology Demonstrations
- Level 4 DC44 - Tactical Logistics
- Level 4 DJ28 - Test Measurement Technology Development
- Level 4 DXXA - Soldier Survivability

Level 3 0603002A - Medical Advanced Technology
- Level 4 D806 - Breast Cancer Research
- Level 4 D810 - Industrial Base/Infectious Disease Vaccines and Drugs
- Level 4 D819 - Field Medical Protection and Human Performance Enhancement - Non-Systems Advanced Development

Level 3 0603003A - Aviation Advanced Technology
- Level 4 D313 - Research Aircraft Systems
- Level 4 D435 - Aircraft Weapons
- Level 4 D436 - Rotary Wing Controls and Rotors
- Level 4 D447 - Aircraft Demonstration Engines
- Level 4 DB38 - Tractor Cone
- Level 4 DB39 - Advanced Distributed Simulation
- Level 4 DB97 - Aircraft Avionics Equipment

Level 3 0603053A - Advanced Command and Control Vehicle
- Level 4 DG23 - ADVANCED COMMAND AND CONTROL VEHICLE

Level 3 0603102A - Materials & Structure Advanced Technology
- Level 4 D071 - COMPONENTS SCALE-UP
- Level 4 DF33 - CAST DUCTILE IRON COMPONENTS
- Level 4 DJ01 - COMBAT ENGINEERING COMPONENTS

Level 3 0603105A - Military HIV Research
- Level 4 DH29 - Military HIV Research

Level 3 0603270A - EW Technology

- Level 4 DK15 - Advanced Communications Electronics Countermeasures Demonstration
- Level 4 DK16 - Non-communications Electronic Countermeasures Technology Demonstration
- Level 4 DK18 - STINGRAY

Level 3 0603308A - Army Missile Defense Sys Integration
- Level 4 Project number unspecified

Level 3 0603313A - Missile & Rocket Advanced Technology
- Level 4 D085 - DEMONSTRATION OF ADVANCED RADAR TECHNIQUES (DART)*
- Level 4 D206 - Missile Simulation
- Level 4 D263 - The Army Combined Arms Weapon System (TACAWS) Technology Demonstration(s)
- Level 4 D271 - Multi-role Survivable Radar
- Level 4 D401 - Insensitive Munitions for Missile Propulsion
- Level 4 D404 - Dual Mode Seeker
- Level 4 D486 - Rapid Force Projection Simulation
- Level 4 D493 - Rapid Force Projection Demonstration
- Level 4 D496 - Enhanced Fiber Optic Guided Missile (EFOG-M) Demonstration

Level 3 0603606A - Landmine Warfare & Barrier Advanced Tech
- Level 4 D006 - Landmine Warfare Development
- Level 4 D608 - Countermine & Barrier Development

Level 3 0603607A - Joint Service Small Arms Program
- Level 4 D627 - Joint Service Small Arms Program (JSSAP)

Level 3 0603640A - Artillery Propellant Development
- Level 4 DB91 - Unicharge

Level 3 0603653A - Advanced Tank Armament System (ATAS)
- Level 4 DB99 - ATAS

Level 3 0603710A - Night Vision Advanced Technology
- Level 4 DK70 - Night Vision Advanced Technology
- Level 4 DK86 - Night Vision, Airborne Systems
- Level 4 DK87 - Night Vision, Combat Vehicles

Level 3 0603747A - Soldier Support and Survivability

Level 3 0603759A - Chem/Bio Defense & Smoke AdvTech
- Level 4 DE83 - Chemical Biological Defense Systems Advanced Technology

Level 3 0603790A - NATO Research & Development

Level 3 0603804A - Logistics and Engineer Equipment - Adv Dev
- Level 4 D266 - Airdrop Equipment Advanced Development
- Level 4 DG01 - Combat Engineer Equipment Advanced Development
- Level 4 DG10 - Advanced Tactical Power Sources Advanced Development
- Level 4 DG11 - Advanced Electrical Energy Concepts Advanced Development
- Level 4 DG14 - Logistics Support Equipment Advanced Development
- Level 4 DK39 - General Support Equipment Advanced Development
- Level 4 DK41 - Petroleum, Oil, and Lubricants (POL) Distribution Equipment Advanced Development

Level 3 0603805A - Combat Service Support Computer System Evaluation and Analysis
- Level 4 D246 - Tactical Communications Systems-Advanced Development

Level 3 0603806A - NBC Defense System - Adv Dev
- Level 4 D601 - NBC Contamination Avoidance Systems

Level 3 0603807A - Medical Systems - Adv Dev
- Level 4 D809 - Medical Biological Defense Drug and Vaccine - Advanced Development

- Level4 D811 - Military HIV Vaccine and Drug - Advanced Development
- Level3 0604630A - Advanced Tank Cannon
  - Level4 DB80 - ATAC AMMO
  - Level4 DB81 - ADVANCED TANK CANNON (ATAC)
- Level3 0604715A - Non-System Training Devices - Eng Dev
  - Level4 D241 - Non-System Training Devices Combined Arms
- Level3 0604741A - Air Defense Command, Control and Intelligence - Eng Dev
  - Level4 D2JT - FAAD C2 Operational Test
- Level3 0604759A - Major T&E Investment
  - Level4 D983 - Major Test and Evaluation Investment - USAKA
  - Level4 D984 - Major Technical Test Instrumentation *
  - Level4 D986 - Major User Test Instrumentation
  - Level4 DC55 - Distributed Development Simulation Technology
- Level3 0604806A - NBC Defense System-Eng Dev
  - Level4 D020 - NBC Contamination Avoidance Systems
  - Level4 DF97 - NBC Decontamination Systems
- Level3 0604807A - Medical Materiel/Medical Biological Defense Equipment - Eng Dev
  - Level4 D849 - Infectious Diseases Drug and Vaccine
- Level3 0604814A - Sense and Destroy Armament Missile - Eng Dev
  - Level4 D644 - Sense and Destroy Armor (SADARM)
- Level3 0605602A - Army Technical Test Instrumentation and Targets
  - Level4 D453 - Technical Test Instrumentation*
  - Level4 D628 - Test Technology & Sustaining Instrumentation
- Level3 0605604A - Survivability/Lethality Analysis
  - Level4 D089 - Aircraft Certification *
  - Level4 D181 - Antiradiation Missile Counter-Countermeasures
  - Level4 D190 - Integrated Analysis
  - Level4 D234 - Close Combat/Fire Support Survivability/Lethality
  - Level4 D235 - Missile Counter-Countermeasure Technology
  - Level4 D267 - Air Defense/Missile Defense Survivability/Lethality
  - Level4 D462 - Technical Vulnerability Reduction
  - Level4 D626 - C4I Survivability
  - Level4 DC10 - Aviation System Survivability/Lethality/Vulnerability
- Level3 0605702A - Meteorological Support to RDT&E Activities
  - Level4 D127 - Meteorological Support to ARL Activities
- Level3 0605801A - Programwide Activities
  - Level4 M881 - RDTE Command/Center/General Administrative Support
  - Level4 MAC3 - Ozone Depleting Chemicals Elimination
  - Level4 MAC4 - Pollution Prevention in Acquisition
- Level3 0605878A - Maintenance and Repair (RPM) - RDT&E
  - Level4 MOYY - Maintenance and Repair - AMC Test Ranges
- Level3 CRADAs

Level2 Department of the Navy

- Level3 0204136N - F/A-18 Squadrons
  - Level4 E2065 - F/A-18 RADAR Upgrade
- Level3 0204311N - Integrated Surveillance System
  - Level4 Project number unspecified

- Level3 0205601N - HARM Improvement
  - Level4 W1780 - Harm Improvement
- Level3 0205604N - Tactical Data Links
  - Level4 P1753 - Link Eleven Improvements
  - Level4 P1977 - Navy JTIDS
  - Level4 P2126 - Multifunctional Information Distribution System
- Level3 0205633N - Aviation Improvements
  - Level4 W1041 - Aircraft Equipment Reliability & Maintainability Improvement Program (AERMIP)
  - Level4 W1355 - Aircraft Engine Component Improvement Program (CIP)
- Level3 0205658N - Navy Science Assistance Program
  - Level4 R0834 - Navy Science Assistance Program (NSAP)
- Level3 0206623M - Marine Corps Ground Combat/Supporting Arms System
  - Level4 C0021 - Assault Amphibious Vehicle 7A1 (AAV7A1)
  - Level4 C1555 - Light Armored Vehicle Program
  - Level4 C1960 - Light Armored Vehicle - Air Defense (LAV-AD)
- Level3 0206624M - Marine Corps Combat Services Support
  - Level4 C0079 - Combat Clothing and Equipment
- Level3 0601152N - In-House Independent Laboratory Res
  - Level4 ADV. MATLS.
  - Level4 INFO. SCI.
  - Level4 OCEAN SCI.
  - Level4 Project number unspecified
  - Level4 SUST. PROG.
- Level3 0601153N - Defense Research Sciences
  - Level4 Project number unspecified
- Level3 0602111N - Surface/Aerospace Surveil/Weapons Tech
  - Level4 Surface/Aerospace Surveillance and Weapons Technology
- Level3 0602122N - Aircraft Technology
  - Level4 Aircraft Technology
- Level3 0602131M - Marine Corps Landing Force Technology
  - Level4 Marine Corps Landing Force Technology
- Level3 0602233N - Readiness, Training, Environ. Quality Tech
  - Level4 Mission Support Technology
- Level3 0602234N - Materials, Electronic & Computer Tech
  - Level4 Materials, Electronics and Computer Technology
- Level3 0602314N - Undersea Surveillance Weapon Tech
  - Level4 Undersea Surveillance and Weapons Technology
- Level3 0602315N - Mine Countermeasure/Mining/Spec Warfare
  - Level4 Mine Countermeasures, Mining and Special Warfare Technology
- Level3 0602435N - Oceanographic & Atmospheric Technology
  - Level4 Oceanographic and Atmospheric Technology
  - Level4 Project number unspecified
- Level3 0603207N - Air/Ocean Tactical Applications
  - Level4 Project number unspecified
  - Level4 X0523 - Air/Ocean Data Assimilation
  - Level4 X2008 - Tactical Ocean Data Assimilation and Prediction

- Level 3 0603216N - Aviation Survivability
  - Level 4 W0584 - A/C Protective Clothing and Devices
  - Level 4 W0592 - A/C & Ordnance Safety
  - Level 4 W1277 - Nuclear Survivable Aircraft (FAANTAEL)
  - Level 4 W1819 - CV A/C Fire Suppression System
- Level 3 0603217N - Air Systems & Weapons Advanced Tech
  - Level 4 R0447 - Weapons Advanced Technology
  - Level 4 R2152 - Advanced Short Takeoff and Vertical Landing (ASTOVL) Demonstrator
  - Level 4 W0447 - ELECTROMAGNETIC RADIATION SOURCE ELIMINATION (ERASE)
  - Level 4 W2185 - Advanced Anti-Radiation Guided Missile (AARGM)
- Level 3 0603238N - Precision Strike & Air Defense
  - Level 4 R2145 - Precision Strike and Air Defense Tech Demos
- Level 3 0603270N - Advanced Electronic Warfare Technology
  - Level 4 E2194 - Electronic Warfare Advanced Technology
- Level 3 0603502N - Surface and Shallow Water Mine Countermeasures
  - Level 4 Project number unspecified
  - Level 4 Q1233 - MCM Improvements
- Level 3 0603506N - Surface Ship Torpedo Defense
  - Level 4 V2045 - Joint US/UK SSTD
- Level 3 0603514N - Ship Combat Survivability
  - Level 4 S1565 - SHIP DAMAGE CONTROL (ADV)
- Level 3 0603555N - Sea Control & Littoral Warfare Tech Demo
  - Level 4 R2142 - Sea Control and Littoral Warfare Technology Demo
- Level 3 0603561N - Advanced Submarine System Development
- Level 3 0603609N - Conventional Munitions
  - Level 4 S0363 - Insensitive Munitions Advanced Development
  - Level 4 U1821 - Conventional Fuze/Warhead Pkg
- Level 3 0603634N - Electromagnetic Effects Protection Development
  - Level 4 S0342 - ELECTROMAGNETIC EFFECTS PROTECTION DEVELOPMENT
- Level 3 0603640M - Marine Corps Adv Tech Demo
  - Level 4 C2080 - Weaponry
  - Level 4 C2118 - Advanced Engine/Propulsion Technology
- Level 3 0603713N - Ocean Engineering Technology Development
  - Level 4 M0099 - Deep Submergence Biomedical Development
- Level 3 0603721N - Environmental Protection
  - Level 4 S0400 - Ordnance Reclamation
- Level 3 0603724N - Navy Energy Program
  - Level 4 R0829 - Energy Conservation (ADV)
  - Level 4 R0838 - Mobility Fuels (ADV)
- Level 3 0603725N - Facilities Improvement
  - Level 4 Y0995 - Naval Facilities Systems
- Level 3 0603747N - Undersea Warfare Advanced Technology
  - Level 4 X1959 - Critical Sea Tests (CST)
- Level 3 0603763N - Warfare Systems Architecture and Engineering
  - Level 4 X1991 - WSA&E
- Level 3 0603785N - Combat Systems Oceanographic Performance Assessment
  - Level 4 Project number unspecified

- Level 3 0603792N - Advanced Technology Transition
  - Level 4 R1889 - Advanced Technology Demonstrations
- Level 3 0603795N - Gun Weapon System Technology
  - Level 4 S2093 - Gun Weapon Systems (WARSHIPS)
- Level 3 0603800N - Joint Strike Advanced Technology Program
- Level 3 0604214N - AV-8B Aircraft - Eng Dev
  - Level 4 H0652 - AV-8B (HARRIER II)
- Level 3 0604217N - S-3 Weapon System Improvement
  - Level 4 H0489 - S-3 WSIP
- Level 3 0604218N - Air/Ocean Equipment Engineering
  - Level 4 R1740 - AIR/OCEAN SURVEY ENGINEERING
- Level 3 0604231N - Tactical Command System
  - Level 4 X2009 - OBU/OSG
- Level 3 0604233N - AFX
  - Level 4 D2129 - A/FX DEVELOPMENT
- Level 3 0604256N - Threat Simulator Development
  - Level 4 E0602 - Electronic Warfare Environment Simulation (ECHO)
- Level 3 0604258N - Target Systems Development
  - Level 4 A0609 - Aerial Target Systems Development
  - Level 4 A0610 - Weapon Systems T&E Training Development/Procurement
  - Level 4 A0611 - Supersonic Sea Skimming Target
- Level 3 0604262N - V-22A
  - Level 4 W2088 - MEDIUM LIFT REPLACEMENT
- Level 3 0604270N - EW Development
  - Level 4 E0556 - EW Counter Response
  - Level 4 E0619 - ASPJ Common Development
  - Level 4 E0638 - Airborne Defensive ECM
  - Level 4 E2175 - Tactical Air Electronic Warfare
  - Level 4 R1882 - Data Link Vulnerability Analysis
- Level 3 0604366N - Standard Missile Improvements
  - Level 4 U0439 - Standard Missile Improvements
  - Level 4 U1632 - AEGIS ER (SM-2 Block IV)
- Level 3 0604567N - Ship Contract Design/Live Fire T&E
  - Level 4 Project number unspecified
- Level 3 0604574N - Navy Tactical Computer Resources
  - Level 4 X1976 - Next Generation Computer Resources
- Level 3 0604603N - Unguided Conventional Air-Launched Weapons
  - Level 4 A2183 - Improved SLAM
  - Level 4 E1341 - Advanced Rocket System
- Level 3 0604710N - Navy Energy Program
  - Level 4 R0371 - Energy Conservation (ENG)
- Level 3 0604719M - Marine Corps Command/Control/Communications Systems
  - Level 4 C2085 - Advanced Field Artillery Tactical Data System (AFATDS)
- Level 3 0604755N - Ship Self Defense
  - Level 4 U0167 - 5 Rolling Airframe Missile
  - Level 4 U2190 - NULKA Decoy
- Level 3 0604759N - Major T&E Investment

- Level4 W2195 - T&E Investment
- Level3 0604777N - Navigation/ID System
  - Level4 X0921 - NAVSTAR GPS Equipment
- Level3 0605152N - Studies and Analysis Support - Navy
  - Level4 R2040 - Foreign Ship and Submarine Vulnerability Program
  - Level4 W2092 - Naval Aviation Studies
- Level3 0605155N - Fleet Tactical Development
  - Level4 R0151 - Intertype Tactical Development and Evaluation
- Level3 0605804N - Technical Information Services
  - Level4 R0835 - Technical Information Services
- Level3 0605853N - Management, Technical & International Support
  - Level4 R0115 - Supreme Allied Commander Atlantic ASW Research Center (SACLANTCE!
  - Level4 R0905 - Naval Warfare Tactical Analysis
- Level3 0605861N - RDT&E Science and Technology Management
  - Level4 R0135 - ONR Science and Technology Management0
  - Level4 R1855 - Science/Engineering Training Support
  - Level4 X0832 - Central Management Support
- Level3 0605862N - RDT&E Instrumentation Modernization
  - Level4 W0566 - NAVAIR Instrumentation and Material Support
- Level3 0605864N - Test and Evaluation Support
  - Level4 W0653 - Naval Air Warfare Center Weapons Division
- Level3 0605865N - Operational Test and Evaluation Capability
  - Level4 R0831 - Operational Test and Evaluation Force Support
- Level3 0605866N - Navy Space and Electronic Warfare (SEW) Support
  - Level4 R0739 - Navy C4I Top Level Requirements

- Level2 Developmental Test and Evaluation
  - Level3 0605130D - Foreign Comparative Testing
    - Level4 Project number unspecified
  - Level3 0605804D - Development Test and Evaluation
    - Level4 920 - Test and Evaluation: Defensewide Support
- Level2 Office of the Secretary of Defense
  - Level3 0305141D - Joint Remotely Piloted Vehicles Program
    - Level4 UNMANNED AERIAL VEHICLES JOINT PROGRAM (UAV) A.
  - Level3 0305190D - C3I Intelligence Programs
    - Level4 P481 - C3I Intelligence Programs
  - Level3 0601103D - University Research Initiatives
    - Level4 Project number unspecified
  - Level3 0601109D - US-JAPAN Management Training
    - Level4 Project number unspecified
  - Level3 0602222D - Counterterror Technical Support
    - Level4 Explosive Detection/Explosive Ordnance Disposal
    - Level4 Surveillance and Threat Assessment
    - Level4 Target Security
  - Level3 0602228D - Historically Black Coll/Univ Science & Eng.
    - Level4 Project number unspecified
  - Level3 0602787D - Medical Technology
    - Level4 P505 - Casualty Management

- Level 4 P510 - Performance Management
- Level 4 P511 - Molecular/Cellular Gene Modulation
- Level 4 P512 - Hazards Analysis
- Level 3 0603714D - Advanced Sensor Applications Program
- Level 4 P-714 - ASAP
- Level 3 0603715D - AIM-9 Consolidated Program
- Level 4 AIM-9 SIDEWINDERA.
- Level 3 0603716D - Strategic Environmental Res Pgm
- Level 4 P470 - Strategic Environmental Research and Development Program (SERDP)
- Level 4 Project number unspecified
- Level 3 0603755D - High Performance Computing Modern. Pgm
- Level 4 Project number unspecified
- Level 3 0603756D - Consolidated DOD Software Initiative
- Level 4 P453 - DOD COMMON PROGRAMMING LANGUAGE (ADA)
- Level 3 0603790D - NATO Research and Development
- Level 4 Project number unspecified
- Level 3 0604771D - Joint Tactical Information Distribution System
- Level 4 P771 - Joint Tactical Information Distribution System (JTIDS) - Class 2/2H/2 M Terminals
- Level 4 P773 - Multi functional Information Distribution System-Low Volume Terminal (MIDS-LVT)
- Level 2 Special Operations Command
- Level 3 1160402BB - Special Operations Advanced Technology Development
- Level 4 P204 - EXPLOSIVE ORDNANCE DISPOSAL FOR LOW-INTENSITY CONFLICT
- Level 3 1160404BB - Special Operations Tactical Systems Development
- Level 4 3284 - SOF AIRCRAFT DEFENSIVE SYSTEMS
- Level 4 S0417 - SEAL SUPPORT SYSTEMS

Level 1 Department of Education

- Level 2 Higher Education
- Level 3 Fund for the Improvement of Postsecondary Education (FIPSE)
- Level 3 International Education & Foreign Language Studies

Level 1 Department of Energy

- Level 2 CRADAs (Cooperative R&D Agreements)
- Level 2 Defense Environmental Restoration & Waste Management
- Level 3 Groundwater & soil cleanup
- Level 3 Other activities
- Level 3 Pollution prevention
- Level 3 Waste retrieval & processing
- Level 2 Energy Conservation
- Level 3 Buildings Sector
- Level 4 Building equipment & materials/Materials and structures
- Level 4 Building equipment & materials/Space conditioning
- Level 4 Building systems design/Best practices
- Level 3 Industry sector
- Level 4 Energy systems/Process heating & cooling
- Level 4 Process efficiency/Chemicals & petroleum refining

- Level 3 Transportation sector
  - Level 4 Alternative fuel utilization/AFV deployment
  - Level 4 Combustion engine R&D/Heavy duty engine
  - Level 4 Transportation materials technology/Propulsion systems materials
- Level 2 Energy Supply
  - Level 3 Basic energy sciences
    - Level 4 Chemical sciences -- Research
    - Level 4 Engineering & geosciences -- Geosciences research
    - Level 4 Extramural awards
    - Level 4 Materials sciences -- Research
  - Level 3 Biological and environmental research
    - Level 4 Environmental processes - Atmospheric chemistry & carbon cycle
    - Level 4 Environmental remediation -- Terrestrial transport
    - Level 4 Life sciences - Health effects
    - Level 4 Life sciences -- Genome
    - Level 4 Life sciences -- Molecular & cellular biology
    - Level 4 Medical applications -- Radioisotope development
  - Level 3 Computational & technology research
  - Level 3 Environment, safety & health
    - Level 4 Laboratory tasks
  - Level 3 Fusion energy
    - Level 4 Inertial fusion energy/Heavy ion beams
    - Level 4 Magnetic fusion energy -- Applied plasma physics/MFE computing
    - Level 4 Magnetic fusion energy -- Confinement sys/Tokamak Fusion Test Reactor (TFTR)
    - Level 4 Magnetic fusion energy -- Confinement sys/Tokamak Physics Experiment (TPX)
    - Level 4 Magnetic fusion energy -- Confinement systems/Advanced toroidal
    - Level 4 Magnetic fusion energy -- Confinement systems/Base toroidal
    - Level 4 Magnetic fusion energy -- Development & technology/Advanced materials
    - Level 4 Magnetic fusion energy -- Development & technology/Fusion systems studies
    - Level 4 Magnetic fusion energy -- Development & technology/Fusion technologies
    - Level 4 Magnetic fusion energy -- Development & technology/ITER
    - Level 4 Magnetic fusion energy -- Development & technology/Plasma technologies
  - Level 3 Nuclear energy
    - Level 4 Advanced reactor/Gas Turbine-Modular Helium Reactor (GT-MHR)
    - Level 4 Advanced reactor/Integral fast reactor/Actinide Recycle
    - Level 4 Light water reactors/Commercial light water reactor
    - Level 4 Soviet design reactor
    - Level 4 Space reactor power systems
  - Level 3 Solar & renewable energy
    - Level 4 Geothermal energy/Geothermal technology development
    - Level 4 High temperature superconductivity
    - Level 4 Solar & renewable energy deployment/Solar international
    - Level 4 Solar thermal/ST electric/Power applications
    - Level 4 Solar thermal/Solar industrial/Solar detoxification
    - Level 4 Wind energy systems/Utility sector/Utility & Industry Program
  - Level 3 University & science education
    - Level 4 Extramural awards

- Level 4 Laboratory science cooperative science ctrs
- Level 4 University programs
- Level 2 Fossil Energy
  - Level 3 Petroleum, coal, gas & cooperative R&D
    - Level 4 Coal -- Advanced clean fuels research/Coal preparation
    - Level 4 Coal -- Advanced research & technology/Components
    - Level 4 Coal -- Advanced research & technology/Tech X-cut/Bioprocessing of coal
    - Level 4 Coal -- Advanced research & technology/Tech X-cut/Coal technology export
    - Level 4 Coal -- Advanced research & technology/Tech X-cut/International program support
    - Level 4 Gas -- Natural gas research/New gas pgm/Exploration & production
    - Level 4 Gas -- Natural gas research/New gas pgm/Utilization
    - Level 4 Petroleum -- Oil technology/Recovery field demonstrations
- Level 2 General Science and Research Activities
  - Level 3 High energy physics
    - Level 4 Facilities operation
    - Level 4 High energy technology
    - Level 4 Physics research
  - Level 3 Nuclear physics
    - Level 4 Low energy nuclear physics
    - Level 4 Medium energy nuclear physics
    - Level 4 Nuclear theory
- Level 2 LDRD (Lab Directed Research & Development)
- Level 2 Materials Support and Other Defense Programs
  - Level 3 Nonproliferation & verification
    - Level 4 On-site monitoring
    - Level 4 Regional monitoring systems
  - Level 3 Nuclear safeguards and security
    - Level 4 Technology and system development/Concept and demonstration development
    - Level 4 Technology and system development/Full scale development
    - Level 4 Technology and system development/Science & technology development
  - Level 3 Special technologies
- Level 2 Reimbursables
- Level 2 Uranium Enrichment
- Level 2 Weapons Activities
  - Level 3 Core stockpile stewardship
    - Level 4 Core research & advanced technology -- Manufacturing technologies
    - Level 4 Programs & initiatives -- Emergency response
    - Level 4 Programs & initiatives -- Spec proj/Educ/Partnerships
    - Level 4 Programs & initiatives -- Stockpile Maintenance Evaluation & Technology
    - Level 4 Programs & initiatives -- Threat assessment & treaty implementation

Level 1 **Department of Health and Human Services**

- Level 2 Agency for Health Care Policy & Research
- Level 2 Centers for Disease Control and Prevention
  - Level 3 Natl Institute for Occupational Safety & Health
    - Level 4 NIOSH Extramural awards
- Level 2 Food & Drug Administration

- Level 3 Biologics
  - Level 4 Product quality control
  - Level 4 Transfusion transmitted diseases
  - Level 4 Viral products
- Level 2 Health Care Financing Administration
- Level 2 National Institutes of Health
  - Level 3 Clinical Center
  - Level 3 John E. Fogarty International Center
    - Level 4 Extramural awards
    - Level 4 Research management & support
  - Level 3 National Cancer Institute
    - Level 4 Cancer biology, detection & diagnosis
    - Level 4 Cancer causation
    - Level 4 Cancer prevention & control
    - Level 4 Cancer treatment
    - Level 4 NCI research manpower development
  - Level 3 National Center for Human Genome Research
    - Level 4 Extramural awards
  - Level 3 National Center for Research Resources
    - Level 4 Biomedical research support (extramural)
    - Level 4 Biomedical research technology (extramural)
    - Level 4 Comparative medicine/Biological models & materials (extramural)
    - Level 4 NCRR clinical research
    - Level 4 R&D Contracts
    - Level 4 Research management & support
  - Level 3 National Eye Institute
    - Level 4 Vision research (extramural)
  - Level 3 National Heart, Lung, & Blood Institute
    - Level 4 Blood diseases & resources (extramural)
    - Level 4 Heart & vascular diseases (extramural)
    - Level 4 Lung diseases (extramural)
  - Level 3 National Inst of Deafness & Other Communicative Disorders
    - Level 4 Deafness & other communication disorders (extramural)
  - Level 3 National Institute for Nursing Research
    - Level 4 Extramural awards
  - Level 3 National Institute of Allergy & Infectious Diseases
    - Level 4 Allergy, immunology & transplantation (extramural)
    - Level 4 Intramural research
    - Level 4 Microbiology & infectious diseases (extramural)
    - Level 4 R&D Contracts
    - Level 4 Research management & support
  - Level 3 National Institute of Arthritis, Musculoskeletal & Skin Diseases
    - Level 4 Arthritis & musculoskeletal & skin diseases (extramural)
  - Level 3 National Institute of Child Health & Human Development
    - Level 4 Intramural research
    - Level 4 Medical rehabilitation research (extramural)
    - Level 4 Population research (extramural)

- Level 4 R&D Contracts
- Level 4 Research for mothers & children (extramural)
- Level 3 National Institute of Dental Research
- Level 4 Intramural research
- Level 4 Oral diseases & disorders (extramural)
- Level 3 National Institute of Diabetes, Digestive & Kidney Diseases
- Level 4 Diabetes, endocrinology & metabolism (extramural)
- Level 4 Digestive diseases & nutrition (extramural)
- Level 4 Intramural research
- Level 4 Kidney disease, urology & hematology (extramural)
- Level 3 National Institute of Environmental Health Sciences
- Level 4 Applied toxicological research and testing
- Level 4 Biological response to environmental agents
- Level 4 Biometry and risk estimation
- Level 4 Intramural research
- Level 4 NIEHS resource & manpower development
- Level 4 R&D Contracts
- Level 4 Superfund worker training program (Funded by EPA, DOT and DOE)
- Level 3 National Institute of General Medical Sciences
- Level 4 Cell biology & biophysics (extramural)
- Level 4 Genetics & developmental biology (extramural)
- Level 4 Minority opportunities in research (extramural)
- Level 4 Pharmacology, physiology & biological chemistry (extramural)
- Level 3 National Institute of Mental Health
- Level 4 Extramural awards
- Level 4 Intramural research
- Level 3 National Institute of Neurological Disorders & Stroke
- Level 4 Biological basis research (extramural)
- Level 4 Clinical research (extramural)
- Level 4 Intramural research
- Level 3 National Institute on Aging
- Level 4 Aging research (extramural)
- Level 4 Intramural research
- Level 3 National Institute on Alcohol Abuse & Alcoholism
- Level 4 Alcohol biomedical & behavioral research (extramural)
- Level 4 Intramural research
- Level 3 National Institute on Drug Abuse
- Level 4 Drug abuse & addiction (extramural)
- Level 4 Intramural research
- Level 3 National Library of Medicine
- Level 4 Extramural awards
- Level 4 R&D Contracts
- Level 3 Office of the Director
- Level 4 Academic Research Enhancement Award Program

- Level 1 **Department of Interior**
- Level 2 Fish & Wildlife Service

- Level 2 Geological Survey - Traditional programs
  - Level 3 Extramural awards for geological surveys-research & data acquisition
  - Level 3 Geological Survey - Formerly the National Biological Service
    - Level 4 Understanding biodiversity
- Level 2 National Park Service

Level 1 Department of Transportation

- Level 2 Federal Highway Administration
  - Level 3 Applied research & technology
  - Level 3 Fundamental properties of asphalt
  - Level 3 Highway research, development &technology
    - Level 4 Structures
  - Level 3 Intelligent transportation systems
- Level 2 Office of the Secretary of Transportation
  - Level 3 Transportation, planning, research & development

Level 1 Department of Veterans Affairs

- Level 2 Medical & Prosthetic Research
  - Level 3 VA Medical Center - (Albany, NY)
  - Level 3 VA Medical Center - (Albuquerque, NM)
  - Level 3 VA Medical Center - (Baltimore, MD)
  - Level 3 VA Medical Center - (Boise, ID)
  - Level 3 VA Medical Center - (Boston, MA)
  - Level 3 VA Medical Center - (Brockton, MA)
  - Level 3 VA Medical Center - (Brooklyn, NY)
  - Level 3 VA Medical Center - (Buffalo, NY)
  - Level 3 VA Medical Center - (Charleston, SC)
  - Level 3 VA Medical Center - (Chicago/Lakeside, IL)
  - Level 3 VA Medical Center - (Cleveland, OH)
  - Level 3 VA Medical Center - (Dallas, TX)
  - Level 3 VA Medical Center - (Dayton, OH)
  - Level 3 VA Medical Center - (Decatur, GA)
  - Level 3 VA Medical Center - (Denver, CO)
  - Level 3 VA Medical Center - (Durham, NC)
  - Level 3 VA Medical Center - (Gainesville, FL)
  - Level 3 VA Medical Center - (Hines, IL)
  - Level 3 VA Medical Center - (Houston, TX)
  - Level 3 VA Medical Center - (Indianapolis, IN)
  - Level 3 VA Medical Center - (Iowa City, IA)
  - Level 3 VA Medical Center - (Jackson, MS)
  - Level 3 VA Medical Center - (Lexington, KY)
  - Level 3 VA Medical Center - (Little Rock, AR)
  - Level 3 VA Medical Center - (Loma Linda, CA)
  - Level 3 VA Medical Center - (Long Beach, CA)
  - Level 3 VA Medical Center - (Madison, WI)
  - Level 3 VA Medical Center - (Memphis, TN)
  - Level 3 VA Medical Center - (Miami, FL)
  - Level 3 VA Medical Center - (Milwaukee, WI)

- Level 3 VA Medical Center - (Minneapolis, MN)
- Level 3 VA Medical Center - (Mountain Home, TN)
- Level 3 VA Medical Center - (Nashville, TN)
- Level 3 VA Medical Center - (New Orleans, LA)
- Level 3 VA Medical Center - (New York, NY)
- Level 3 VA Medical Center - (Northport, NY)
- Level 3 VA Medical Center - (Oklahoma City, OK)
- Level 3 VA Medical Center - (Omaha, NE)
- Level 3 VA Medical Center - (Palo Alto, CA)
- Level 3 VA Medical Center - (Philadelphia, PA)
- Level 3 VA Medical Center - (Phoenix, AZ)
- Level 3 VA Medical Center - (Pittsburgh/US, PA)
- Level 3 VA Medical Center - (Pleasant Hill, CA)
- Level 3 VA Medical Center - (Portland, OR)
- Level 3 VA Medical Center - (Providence, RI)
- Level 3 VA Medical Center - (Reno, NV)
- Level 3 VA Medical Center - (Richmond, VA)
- Level 3 VA Medical Center - (Salt Lake City, UT)
- Level 3 VA Medical Center - (San Antonio, TX)
- Level 3 VA Medical Center - (San Diego, CA)
- Level 3 VA Medical Center - (San Francisco, CA)
- Level 3 VA Medical Center - (Seattle, WA)
- Level 3 VA Medical Center - (Sepulveda, CA)
- Level 3 VA Medical Center - (Syracuse, NY)
- Level 3 VA Medical Center - (Tampa, FL)
- Level 3 VA Medical Center - (Temple, TX)
- Level 3 VA Medical Center - (Tucson, AZ)
- Level 3 VA Medical Center - (Washington, DC)
- Level 3 VA Medical Center - (West Haven, CT)
- Level 3 VA Medical Center - (West Los Angeles/Wadsworth, CA)
- Level 3 VA Medical Center - (White River Jct, VT)
- Level 3 VA Medical Center - (Wichita, KS)

Level 1 **Environmental Protection Agency**

- Level 2 Research and Development
  - Level 3 Air quality
  - Level 3 Multimedia research
  - Level 3 Radiation
  - Level 3 Toxic substances
  - Level 3 Water quality

Level 1 **National Aeronautics and Space Administration**

- Level 2 Academic Programs
  - Level 3 Minority university research & education
    - Level 4 Graduate student researchers program/Underrepresented minority focus
    - Level 4 Historically black colleges and universities (HBCU)
    - Level 4 Other minority universities
    - Level 4 Undergraduate student researchers program/Underrepressented minority focus

- Level 2 Life and Microgravity Science
  - Level 3 Aerospace medicine and occupational health
  - Level 3 Life sciences flight program/Centrifuge
  - Level 3 Life sciences flight program/Space station utilization program
  - Level 3 Life sciences research and analysis/Research and analysis
  - Level 3 Microgravity science research and analysis
  - Level 3 Space station payload facilities
    - Level 4 Life science facilities
- Level 2 Mission to Planet Earth
  - Level 3 EOS data information system
  - Level 3 Earth observing system (EOS)
    - Level 4 Chemistry
    - Level 4 PM Series
  - Level 3 Earth probes
    - Level 4 Total ozone mapping spectrometer (TOMS)
    - Level 4 Tropical rainfall measuring mission (TRMM)
  - Level 3 Modeling & data analysis
    - Level 4 Biogeochemistry & geophysics
    - Level 4 Physical climate & hydrologic systems
  - Level 3 Payload and instrument development
  - Level 3 Process studies
    - Level 4 Ecosystem dynamics & biogeochemical cycles
    - Level 4 Solid earth science
- Level 2 Payload & utilization support
  - Level 3 Advanced projects
- Level 2 Space Access & Technology
  - Level 3 Advanced space transportation
    - Level 4 Technology assessment and development
- Level 2 Space Safety, Reliability & Quality Assurance
- Level 2 Space Science
  - Level 3 Advanced x-ray astrophysics facility development
  - Level 3 Discovery development
  - Level 3 Explorer development
  - Level 3 Mission operations & data analysis
  - Level 3 Payloads & instrument development
  - Level 3 Suborbital program
  - Level 3 Supporting research & technology
    - Level 4 Information systems
    - Level 4 Planetary R&T
    - Level 4 Space physics & astrophysics
- Level 2 Space Tracking & Data Acquisition
- Level 2 Space station
  - Level 3 Flight Hardware

Level 1 **National Science Foundation**

- Level 2 Biological Sciences (BIO)
  - Level 3 Biological instrumentation & resources (BIR)

- Level 4 Biological instrumentation & resources - Other
- Level 4 Databases, software development & comp
- Level 4 Instrumentation & instrument development
- Level 4 Living stock collections

Level 3 Environmental biology (DEB)
- Level 4 Ecology
- Level 4 Ecosystems studies
- Level 4 Environmental biology - Other
- Level 4 Long-term studies in environmental biology
- Level 4 Population biology
- Level 4 Systematics

Level 3 Integrative biology & neuroscience (IBN)
- Level 4 Animal behavior
- Level 4 Animal developmental mechanisms
- Level 4 Computational neuroscience
- Level 4 Ecological & evolutionary phys
- Level 4 Integrative animal biology
- Level 4 Integrative biology & neuroscience - Other
- Level 4 Integrative plant biology
- Level 4 Neuroendrocrinology

Level 3 Molecular & cellular biosciences (MCB)
- Level 4 Cellular organization
- Level 4 Eukaryotic genetics
- Level 4 Metabolic biochemistry
- Level 4 Microbial genetics
- Level 4 Molecular biochemistry
- Level 4 Molecular biophysics
- Level 4 Signal transduction & regulation

Level 2 Computer & Information Science & Engineering (CSE)

Level 3 Computer & computation research (CCR)
- Level 4 Number, symbol & geometric comp
- Level 4 Operating systems & systems software
- Level 4 Programming languages & compilers
- Level 4 Software engineering

Level 3 Information, robotics & intelligent systems (IRI)
- Level 4 Information technology & organizations
- Level 4 Interactive systems
- Level 4 Robotics & machine intelligence

Level 3 Microelectronic information processing systems (MIP)
- Level 4 Microelectric systems architecture

Level 3 Networking & communications research & infrastructure (NCR)
- Level 4 Communications research
- Level 4 NSFNET
- Level 4 Networking research

Level 2 Education & Human Resources (EHR)

Level 3 EPSCOR (OSR)

Level 3 Graduate education & research development (GER)

- Level 3 Human resource development (HRD)
- Level 3 Research, evaluation & dissemination (RED)
- Level 3 Undergraduate education (DUE)

Level 2 Engineering (ENG)

- Level 3 Bioengineering & environmental systems (BES)
  - Level 4 Bioengineering & environmental systems - Other
  - Level 4 Biomedical engineering
  - Level 4 Environmental engineering systems
  - Level 4 Ocean engineering systems
- Level 3 Chemical & transport systems (CTS)
  - Level 4 Combustion & thermal plasmas
  - Level 4 Interfacial, transport & thermodynamic processes
  - Level 4 Kinetics & catalysis
  - Level 4 Particulate & multi-phase processes
  - Level 4 Separation & purification processes
  - Level 4 Thermal transport & thermal processes
- Level 3 Civil & mechanical systems (CMS)
  - Level 4 Architectural & mechanical systems
  - Level 4 Civil & mechanical systems - Other
  - Level 4 Dynamic systems & control
  - Level 4 Earthquake systems integration
  - Level 4 Geomechanical/Geotech & geo-environmental systems
  - Level 4 Large structural & building systems
  - Level 4 Natural & man-made hazard mitigation
  - Level 4 Siting & geotechnical systems
  - Level 4 Structural systems
  - Level 4 Structural systems & construction processes
  - Level 4 Surface engineering tribology
- Level 3 Design, manufacture & industrial innovation (DMI, includes SBIR)
  - Level 4 Computer integrated engineering
  - Level 4 Engineering design
  - Level 4 Manufacturing machines & equipment
  - Level 4 Materials processing & manufacture
  - Level 4 Production systems
  - Level 4 SBIR-Phase I
- Level 3 Directorate-level awards
- Level 3 Electrical & communications systems (ECS)
  - Level 4 Electrical & communications systems - Other
  - Level 4 Electronic devices
  - Level 4 Lightwave technology
  - Level 4 Microelectromechanical research
  - Level 4 Neuroengineering
  - Level 4 Power systems
  - Level 4 Systems theory
- Level 3 Engineering education & centers (EEC)
  - Level 4 Engineering education & centers - Other
  - Level 4 Industry/University cooperative research centers

- Level 2 Geosciences (GEO)
  - Level 3 Atmospheric sciences (ATM)
    - Level 4 Aeronomy
    - Level 4 Atmospheric chemistry
    - Level 4 Atmospheric sciences - Other
    - Level 4 Climate dynamics program
    - Level 4 Large-scale dynamic meteorology
    - Level 4 Magnetospheric physics
    - Level 4 Mesoscale dynamic meteorology
    - Level 4 Physical meteorology
    - Level 4 Solar-terrestrial
  - Level 3 Earth sciences (EAR)
    - Level 4 Continental dynamics
    - Level 4 Education & human resources
    - Level 4 Geology & paleontology
    - Level 4 Geophysics
    - Level 4 Hydrologic sciences
    - Level 4 Instrumentation & facilities
    - Level 4 Petrology & geochemistry
    - Level 4 Tectonics
  - Level 3 Ocean sciences (OCE)
    - Level 4 Biological oceanography
    - Level 4 Chemical oceanography
    - Level 4 International support
    - Level 4 Marine geology & geophysics
    - Level 4 Ocean - Other
    - Level 4 Ocean drilling
    - Level 4 Ocean special programs
    - Level 4 Physical oceanography
- Level 2 Mathematical & Physical Sciences (MPS)
  - Level 3 Astronomical sciences (AST)
    - Level 4 Advanced technologies & instruments
    - Level 4 Extragalactic astronomy & cosmology
    - Level 4 Galactic astronomy
    - Level 4 Planetary astronomy
    - Level 4 Special programs in astronomy
    - Level 4 Stellar astronomy & astrophysics
  - Level 3 Chemistry (CHE)
    - Level 4 Analytical separation & measures
    - Level 4 Chemistry - Other
    - Level 4 Physical inorganic
    - Level 4 Projects
    - Level 4 Structure & reactivity
    - Level 4 Synthesis
    - Level 4 Synthetic inorganic
    - Level 4 Unimolecular processes
  - Level 3 Materials research (DMR)

- Level4 Condensed matter physics
- Level4 Materials theory
- Level4 Metals, ceramics & electrical materials
- Level4 National facilities and instrumentation
- Level4 Solid-state chemistry & polymers

Level3 Mathematical sciences (DMS)

- Level4 Applied mathematics
- Level4 Classical analysis
- Level4 Computational mathematics
- Level4 Foundations
- Level4 Geometric analysis
- Level4 Infrastructure
- Level4 Modern analysis
- Level4 Probability
- Level4 Statistics

Level3 Physics (PHY)

- Level4 Atomic & molecular physics
- Level4 Elementary particle accelerator users
- Level4 Elementary particle cosmic rays & other
- Level4 Gravitational theory
- Level4 Heavy ion nuclear science
- Level4 Intermediate energy nuclear science
- Level4 Low energy nuclear science
- Level4 Physics - Other
- Level4 Theoretical physics

Level2 Social, Behavioral & Economic Sciences (SBE)

Level3 International cooperative scientific activities (INT)

- Level4 Africa, Near East & South Asia
- Level4 Americas
- Level4 East Asia & Pacific
- Level4 Eastern Europe
- Level4 India
- Level4 International activities - Other
- Level4 Japan
- Level4 Research-foreign centers of excellence
- Level4 Western Europe

Level3 Social, behavioral & economic research (SES)(SBR)

- Level4 Archaeology
- Level4 Archaeometry
- Level4 Cultural anthropology
- Level4 Decision risk & management science
- Level4 Economics
- Level4 Ethics & values studies
- Level4 Geography
- Level4 Human cognition & perception
- Level4 Law & social sciences
- Level4 Linguistics

Level4 Methods, measures & statistics in social science
Level4 Physical anthropology
Level4 Political science
Level4 Research on science & technology
Level4 Science & technology studies
Level4 Social psychology
Level4 Sociology
Level4 Systematic anthropological collection
Level2 U.S. Polar Research Programs (DPP, OPP)

Level1 **Nuclear Regulatory Commission**
Level2 Reactor Safety Research
Level3 Reactor regulation

Level1 **Smithsonian Institution**
Level2 Arts & Humanitites Programs (Museum-based research)
Level3 Arthur M. Sackler Gallery/Freer Gallery of Art
Level3 Cooper-Hewitt Museum
Level3 National Museum of African Art
Level2 Science Programs
Level3 International environmental science program
Level3 Migratory Birds Center
Level3 National Museum of Natural History (NMNH)
Level3 National Zoological Park
Level3 Smithsonian Astrophysical Observatory

A more detailed report including budget authority and obligation information for all Federal Organizations involved in the specified activity/area is also available.

Main Query Screen	Save Current Query	Glossary of Terms	RaDiUS Information	Help	Show Query Criteria
Query Summary	View by Fed Org	View by Award/Task	Download		

Last session activity was at **Wed Mar 19 17:41** Pacific Time
User fossum started session 20365 at Wed Mar 19 17:37
*This is **RaDiUS** version 1.61-production. If you have questions or comments about **RaDiUS**, please send mail to radius@rand.org or use this form.*